THE PASTOR AND THE PEOPLE, REVISED

THE PASTOR AND THE PEOPLE

Revised

Lyle E. Schaller

ABINGDON PRESS / Nashville

THE PASTOR AND THE PEOPLE, REVISED

Library of Congress Cataloging-in-Publication Data

SCHALLER, LYLE E.
 The pastor and the people.
 Includes bibliographical references.
 1. Pastoral theology. 2. Theology, Practical. I. Title.
BV4011.S33   1986   254   86-7852

ISBN 0-687-30135-1 (pbk.: alk. paper)

Portions of this book are based on material which has been previously published. Grateful acknowledgment is made for permission to use portions of the following: "Picking the Pastor for the Downtown Church," by Lyle Schaller, copyright 1970 Church Management, Inc. Reprinted by permission from the January 1970 issue of *The Clergy Journal;* "What Are the Priorities?" by Lyle Schaller. This material first appeared in the May 1972 issue of the *Christian Ministry* magazine, reprinted with the permission of the Christian Century Foundation.

BOOK DESIGN BY JOHN ROBINSON

MANUFACTURED BY THE PARTHENON PRESS AT NASHVILLE, TENNESSEE, UNITED STATES OF AMERICA

to
Jane Follmer Zekoff

CONTENTS

THE PASTOR AND THE PEOPLE, REVISED

INTRODUCTION

T his book has been written on the assumption that individuals can learn from the experiences of other people in similar situations.

Any resemblance between the ideas, experiences, and lessons described in these pages and what has actually happened to living people is *not a coincidence*. Everything in this book is taken from what has happened in some parish or to some pastor during the past several years. The names have been changed, to repeat the familiar disclaimer, to protect the innocent, to reduce the chance of any personal embarrassment, and to eliminate the possibility of creating mail for someone else to answer. In many cases the dialogue that is presented was taken from notes made when the event described was actually occurring. Obviously, many experiences from scores of different parishes in several different denominations have been compressed together in this review of the experiences of Pastor Don Johnson's eleven years at St. John's Church.

This book is directed at three overlapping audiences. The initial audience consists of lay leaders in congregations that are about to seek a new pastor and ministers who are in the process of moving to a new pastorate. From a ministerial perspective this process begins with the thought that marks the possibility of moving while with the lay leadership it often begins with the realization that "our pastor is leaving us and we will have to find a successor."

Four of the first five chapters are directed at those lay leaders who have the basic responsibility for choosing a new minister. One of those first five chapters and parts of the other four are directed at the minister who may be moving to a new parish.

Another method of describing this initial audience is to say it includes all the persons involved in the courtship, marriage, and honeymoon period that arises when a parish and a new pastor come together.

The second audience to which this book is directed is composed of both the laity and the clergy in those congregations in which the honeymoon period following the arrival of the new minister is past, but where there remains an open and receptive climate for the introduction of new ideas.

This second audience obviously is the larger of these first two, and one purpose of the book is to encourage both lay leaders and ministers to take a fresh look at what they are doing and how they are doing it in the light of the experiences of other congregations. Sometimes a premature urge of the minister to look for greener pastures elsewhere or of lay leadership to seek new pastoral leadership can be responded to most creatively by their working together to re-evaluate the work of the parish, rather than looking for a new team or seeking a new manager. Hopefully several of the chapters may provide a frame of reference for this re-evaluation and chapters 5, 6, 7, 9, 11, 13, and 16 were written specifically to provide a conceptual framework for the reappraisal.

The third audience to whom this volume is addressed should be too busy to be reading a book, but, given the world as it is, many of them do have the time and may prefer reading to traveling. This third audience is composed of local church leaders who are interested in what other congregations are doing, and who are sure that if they had the chance to go and visit other congregations, they could pick up many insights and ideas that would be helpful to their parish.

They are absolutely correct in that basic assumption. There is much that local church leaders can learn from visiting other parishes and talking with the people there. Such a procedure is far superior to reading a book. However, not every parish leader who believes this has the opportunity to visit other churches.

For the past quarter century I have had the enviable privilege of visiting from one to three hundred congregations annually. Some of these visits are for only an hour or two; most are for a day or two or three; and a few, for four or five or six days.

The material in this book is drawn from those experiences with congregations, which represent three dozen denominations and religious bodies in all parts of the United States and Canada. Out of these experiences have come the incidents, ideas, insights, lessons, and illustrations that are recounted on the following pages.

The first chapter is drawn from the experience of working with a number of search or call or pastor-parish relations committees, and from the observations of denominational executives who are responsible for pastoral placement. The basic intent of this chapter is to suggest the idea of developing a systematic agenda of concerns that will help the lay leadership in a parish as they participate in the process of selecting a new pastor. The use of such a systematic approach will tend to bring to the surface those subjects that either the parish leaders or the prospective pastor believe are "nonnegotiable." The earlier these are identified, the better for everyone concerned.

The second chapter looks at the same process, but from the perspective of a prospective new pastor, while the third chapter suggests a procedure for surfacing and discussing the varying points of view about the priorities on the new minister's time and talent.

One of the most neglected concepts in the pastoral placement process is the occasional need for an interim pastor to bridge the transition between what was and what is yet to come in a parish. Some of the situations in which an interim pastor may be advisable are identified in the fourth chapter.

The fifth chapter reviews several dimensions of the "compensation package." The most obvious of the four is the economic compensation. The other three are satisfactions, expectations, and housing.

The subject of satisfactions, or psychic rewards, is important to many laypersons and clergy, and that is discussed in the sixth chapter. This chapter also marks the beginning of the second section of this volume, which is concerned with the practice of ministry after the new pastor has arrived.

Every pastor has the choice of learning from his or her own experiences and relying on the passage of time to build up an inventory of skills gained from experience, *or* of exploiting the experiences of others to build up those skills at a faster pace, The seventh chapter should be of interest to those who prefer the second of these alternatives and who seek to profit from the experiences of others.

Conventional wisdom suggests that a newly arrived pastor should "take it easy," "size up the lay of the land," and "get acquainted with the people" during that first year. In one out of four situations this is good advice. In at least three out of four cases, however, it is inadequate or bad advice. A more productive approach to the first year is suggested in the eighth chapter.

One of the changes in our society since 1950 is that today we often hire people to do what once was done by volunteers. One result is that today many churches are really understaffed as they seek to meet the needs of people. Suggestions for staffing in order to expand program and outreach can be found in the ninth chapter.

One of the problems that often disturbs the thinking of today's leaders is the gradual disappearance of men and women who once were very active leaders, have not changed their place of residence, but now rarely can be seen around the church. The tenth chapter contains both diagnostic and prescriptive comments on this phenomenon.

It is easy to oversimplify the decision-making processes in the parish, and the eleventh chapter offers one approach that may help to provide a clearer understanding of how others view what is happening. The process described in this chapter has been used in scores of congregations and invariably has provided material for productive discussion on the various influences on the decision-making process in those congregations.

One cause of anxiety in thousands of congregations is the gradual decline in numbers. This is an enormous subject, but one beginning point in this day when the number of church shoppers is growing so rapidly is to look at the number of first-time visitors. How can that number be increased? This is the focal point of the twelfth chapter.

A countless number of debates have been carried on over the importance of a church kitchen. This issue is too important to overlook and suggestions are offered in the thirteenth chapter on how to determine which congregations will find a church kitchen to be of real value and why.

The law of averages applies to churches, as well as to other institutions in our society, and several of the ways cultural patterns influence the nature of ministry are described in the fourteenth chapter.

Much has been written about church renewal, church growth and the need for churches to expand their ministry in response to the changing needs of people. The one question that rarely is asked is, What if we try something new and it works? The answer is that it will change the dynamics of congregational life. The nature and the impact of some of the price tags of success are discussed in the fifteenth chapter.

Two groups of people who often are taken for granted, exploited, and expected to serve without recognition are (a) the workers in the preschool department of the Sunday school and (b) women married to pastors. The sixteenth chapter comments on the second of these two groups.

Sooner or later every minister leaves to become the predecessor of a new minister. Some of the obligations that go with the role of predecessor are described in the concluding chapter.

Those readers with a strong interest in the vocation of parish pastors can view this as the first of a 5-volume series directed specifically at the pastoral ministry. This volume follows the career of the Reverend Mr. Donald Johnson through an eleven-year pastorate. Another volume, *Activating the Passive Church*, focusses more narrowly on a creative response to the matter of passivity in a congregation. A third volume, *Survival Tactics in the Parish*, was written for those ministers interested in a long pastorate with suggestions on how to survive some of the pitfalls that too often create short pastorates. The fourth volume in this series, *Looking in the Mirror*, offers a series of procedures, guidelines, and criteria for congregational self-appraisal. One theme is a conceptual frame of reference, to help both the clergy and the laity identify the distinctive characteristics of the congregation of which they are a part. The final volume, which will follow the career of Don Johnson as he leaves St. John's to become the senior minister of a large congregation, remains to be completed. All five volumes rest on the common assumption that the health of the Christian churches today is not dependent on the impact of books written by sinful human beings, but rather is continuing evidence that God is alive and at work in His world, in His churches, and in the lives of His children.

Ideally this introduction would include a list of the hundreds of exceptionally able, remarkably dedicated, and unusually creative pastors and lay leaders from whom so much has been "borrowed" for this volume. There are two reasons for not mentioning them. The more obvious is the lack of space. The second is an inadequate note-taking system, which guarantees that the publication of such a list also would produce some embarrassing omissions. It is easier and safer simply to say to all who have contributed to the contents of this volume, "Thank you!"

This revised edition is dedicated to an exceptionally gifted, a remarkably creative, and a highly competent pastor of whose many predecessors I am one.

ONE

PICKING
A NEW
PASTOR

I f you ask me, I believe we should look for a new minister who is no older than thirty-five," suggested Jack Peterson. "If we can find a young minister, maybe we can reach some of the young couples in the community who don't like to go to any church."

"Normally I would be inclined to agree with you," replied Betty White, "but I think in our situation the number-one requirement is for a pastor who has the ability to bring people together and to help a congregation function as a unified organization."

"Those are important characteristics," commented the man who later was to become the chairman of this committee at St. John's, "but I think we need a pastor who can be a leader, who can give direction to this parish, and who can help us move ahead."

"You're talking about a leadership style that can be pretty authoritarian at times," interjected Everett Wright. "I was talking to Paul Peters from the denominational headquarters the other day, and he commented on a remarkable similarity between the attitudes and practices of the minister fresh out of seminary and the pastor who is only a few years from retirement. In both cases, according to Dr. Peters, each minister has a self-centered agenda and doggedly sticks to it, regardless of the desires or needs of the congregation. Now I hear some of you saying that we should look for a pastor who, regardless of age, comes in with his or her own agenda and forces it on us. I can't support that. I think we need a minister who is able and willing to help us develop an agenda based on the needs of this congregation and to work from that agenda, rather than imposing an agenda on us."

"Now wait a minute, Everett," responded the advocate of strong leadership, "we're not so far apart. You're saying what I was trying to say. We need someone who can give leadership and help get this parish moving. We're stuck on dead center. Church attendance is going down, our income has just about levelled off, interest in the church is dropping fast, the Sunday school is sick, the women's organization is dying, the men's club is dead. That's our agenda!"

"You've just described some of the reasons Pastor Case decided to move to another church," replied Jack Peterson. "Do you think we should expect that simply getting a new pastor will solve all those problems?"

"I don't expect a new minister to solve all those problems without any help," said the advocate of strong leadership, "but I firmly believe our next pastor should be able to help us identify our problems, figure out the causes, and lead us in solving them. In baseball the losing team gets a new manager. St. John's is a losing team today. We need a new manager!"

"I read a good definition of an attractive style of leadership," interjected Betty White. "Robert K. Greenleaf says that the key element in a servant style of leadership is foresight. He says a leader should be able to look beyond today and see the probable consequences of each alternative course of action.[1] I think that's what we need here, someone who can be a part of a leadership team in this parish and yet, at the same time, have a kind of detachment that enables the pastor to look at what we're doing with a more critical eye than any of us can bring to the situation."

As the members of St. John's Church continued to talk about a replacement for their pastor, who had announced his resignation, it became increasingly obvious that what they were seeking was a set of guidelines they could use in picking the next pastor.

Perhaps a better way to approach this subject is to think in terms of a common agenda that can be helpful to all parties in this process. These individuals include the representatives from the parish, the regional denominational executive responsible for pastoral placement, and the prospective pastors or candidates.

Each one of these three parties has a personal agenda. For the parish leaders it may be getting the best minister available; it may be a deliberate decision to look for someone who can pour oil on troubled waters; it may be the hope that the new pastor will solve all their problems unilaterally; or it may be simply to find the best person available for the least amount of money.

The denominational executive in the regional judicatory usually has several vacancies to worry about and an even larger number of ministers wanting to move. In one case that executive may be allocating large quantities of time and energy in an effort to find the "right" minister for a vacant pulpit at a crucial point in one congregation's history. In another, it may be an effort to fit a square peg into a round hole—and hoping it will not pop out for a year or two, until more time can be given to that parish. In yet another case, the regional leader may conclude that a particular parish, after a succession of three outstanding pastors, has an obligation to accept a minister who is more lovable than competent or who is neither competent nor lovable, but needs to leave where he or she is now.

The third party in these negotiations is the prospective new pastor. That individual's agenda may be dominated by a desire to find a parish that fully challenges his or her capabilities or by a very strong desire to leave what no longer is an appropriate match or by the desire to move to a different section of the country or by the need for an increase in compensation or by the longing for a new and different type of pastoral experience or by a desire to serve "one more church" before retirement.

All too often these three parties discuss the selection of the next pastor for a parish without the aid of a common agenda.

Each tends to wait more or less patiently for "my agenda" to move to the forefront in the discussions and does not give adequate attention to the items that should be on all three agendas, but in reality may not be on any of them.

It may be more effective to develop a basic, common agenda for all three parties to use as a beginning point in the discussions than to attempt to merge these three agendas into one.

The following list is suggested not as a universal agenda that can be used in all situations, but rather as a checklist or a supplementary agenda to be used in addition to the lists each party brings to the discussions.

1. The item that should be at the top of the agenda is *purposes*. What is the purpose of this congregation, meeting at this geographical location at this point in history? What do the members believe the Lord is calling their parish to do and to be? All parties should be prepared and willing to discuss purpose in terms of function, program, mission, and role, as well as in terms of traditional theological cliches.

If the pulpit committee does not bring up this matter, or if they fumble when the prospective candidate raises questions about purpose, the candidate would be well advised to pursue the subject vigorously. It may turn out that if the candidate does accept the call, the first task will be to help the congregation review and redefine this question of purpose and role.

On the other hand, the pulpit committee should be wary of any prospective candidate who does not raise questions about how this parish defines its purpose and explains its reason for being.

2. Program is important but it is of secondary importance. "Form follows function" is an expression used frequently by architects. Churchmen should recognize that, similarly, program is an outgrowth of purpose.

If, in the inevitable discussion on the program of the church, all conversation by the pulpit committee is directed to the content of the program and to the importance of "making it go," the pastor should push the committee to describe how the program relates to purpose and why these priorities are being stated in this sequence. For example, if the committee places a great emphasis on youth ministries, the candidate would be well advised to probe why youth are being given such high priority. Frequently, strong emphasis on youth, visitation or calling, preaching, and music are signs of a passive congregation.[2]

The pulpit committee should expect to be asked these questions. If they do not hear them, they should inquire how the pastor sees this relationship between purpose and program.

3. All parties should present a strong orientation to the future. This is extremely important in the case of certain types of churches. If the pulpit committee appears to be out to recruit a minister who has the determination and ability to turn the clock back to 1927 or 1955, the prospective candidate may find this to be a good time to terminate the interview.

Likewise, if the minister being interviewed turns out to have a strong orientation to yesterday, the pulpit committee probably should make the interview as brief as possible. This may be the kind of minister the committee members want, but it almost certainly is not the kind of pastor this church will need in the 1990s.

4. An openness to change, creativity, and innovation is another item that each party should look for in the other.

Unless this characteristic is present in *both* the new pastor and the leadership of the congregation, the unique opportunities for innovation that are present during the "honeymoon period" that usually accompanies the coming of a new pastor may be lost. Conventional wisdom suggests a new pastor usually should spend the honeymoon period getting acquainted and building up a feeling of mutual trust before becoming involved in proposals for change. In today's church there may not be time for that luxury. That first year may turn out to be the best—and occasionally the last—opportunity for creative innovation.

5. The present *and future* clientele should be on both agendas. Before seeking a new pastor the congregation should look very carefully at its membership and constituency, both present and potential. Too often this is not done or the entire focus is on the present membership or the current population

(or both) living near the meeting place. It is increasingly common that most of tomorrow's potential new members do not live within walking distance of the meeting place. It is far more likely they live a mile or two or more away. The pulpit committee offers a description of, and the prospective pastor bases a response on, a stereotyped impression of the clientele that may correspond more to the past than to the present and bears little relationship to the future.

Three current trends can be cited to illustrate this point. The first is that the vast majority of Protestant congregations see themselves as a "family church" and this often is defined to mean husband-wife couples living together with children under age eighteen at home. In recent years that segment of the adult population of the United States has actually decreased in numbers and now includes fewer than one-third of all adults in the nation. Moreover, as the number of widowed women has nearly doubled since 1940 (and the number of widowed men has declined slightly), there has been a strong national trend for these widowed women to move out of the central city and into the suburbs. One reason for this is that a rapidly increasing percentage of widows, due to Social Security and other pension systems, can afford to live alone.

A second trend is that today many young adults are theologically far more conservative than their parents. This has been a major factor in the numerical decline of those denominations that have operated on the assumption that each generation will be more liberal than previous generations.

A third trend is a reflection of the fact that the primary point of socialization has moved from the neighborhood to the workplace. This has had a severe negative impact on those congregations that continue to see themselves as neighborhood churches or geographical parishes.

If the committee has failed to identify the principal societal trends that will influence the future of that congregation, the candidate may be well advised to begin to ask questions about contemporary reality. Too often the committee is seeking a new minister who will turn back the clock.

6. One of the most significant changes occurring in many

churches is a division of opinion over professionalism. This can be seen in the development of a volunteer choir to replace the paid choir, in the disappearance of the pastor who "ran the church," and in the replacement of the second or third ordained minister of the large churches with two or three or four part-time lay specialists who have not been professionally trained for that particular program responsibility.

There is still nothing resembling a consensus on this point among either laymen or clergymen. Therefore it is extremely important that there be a frank exchange of views and values on this question. Is the congregation seeking a person who will be their leader and see that every function of the church is carried out with professional skill and finesse? Does the committee expect an increasing role for lay volunteers or do the members of the committee concur with the general trend that what once was done by volunteers often today is the responsibility of paid staff members? Will the secretarial work be done by the pastor? By volunteers? By a paid secretary? Who will oversee and expand the ministry of education? Volunteers? A full-time professionally trained staff person? Or a part-time lay person who is not professionally trained? These and similar questions are especially relevant for middle-sized congregations that are convinced they have the potential for substantial numerical growth.

7. Nearly every pulpit committee is interested in the competence of a prospective candidate as a preacher. Not infrequently this is the first item on their agenda.

While preaching is important, and it is far more important today than it was in the 1960s, the pulpit committee would do well to enlarge this item on their agenda to the larger subject of corporate worship. How competent is this minister as a leader of worship? What is the candidate's attitude on the number of worship services that should be held each week? Is this minister primarily interested in one large crowd each Sunday morning, or is the candidate open to scheduling two or three or four services each Sunday in order to increase the total number of people who will share in the worship experience? What is the candidate's attitude toward innovation and variety in worship?

The minister who is considering a call to a church also should be asking these and similar questions of the pulpit committee. What is expected of the new minister as a worship leader? Do these expectations coincide with what appears to be the contemporary need? If this congregation does or should offer two worship experiences on Sunday morning, should one be substantially different from the other? Or should they be carbon copies? Will the chancel choir be expected to sing at one or at both? How frequently will people have the opportunity to share in the Lord's Supper?

8. A subject rarely explored adequately in these discussions is the length of the pastorate of the pastor who is being replaced. If the new minister is following a pastor who served the church for two decades or more, the chances are four out of five that he or she will encounter problems that may greatly shorten the new minister's tenure.

While the exceptions to this generalization merit acknowledgment, approximately three-fourths of the pastors who serve the same congregation for over twenty years leave a legacy that greatly handicaps their successors. This legacy often includes a limited capacity of the congregation to adapt to change and the repeated references to how "Dr. Jones did that" or how "Dr. Smith always did this." This legacy also often involves a loyalty to the beloved pastor rather than to Christ and his church, an orientation to the past rather than to the present, and, most serious of all, a definition of purpose that has increasingly emphasized survival and a ministry to the members. This legacy often includes a growing neglect of evangelism, prophetic witness, and involvement in mission in the community.

Here again is a subject that should be on both agendas, and frank discussion should be encouraged.

9. The selection of a new pastor should be accompanied by a review of the compensation for the minister. One part of this package that may be overlooked is the sabbatical leave for study or travel, or simply for rest and rehabilitation. A growing number of churches are including a sabbatical as a part of the agreement in calling a new minister. A few are going beyond

this and providing unusual opportunities for the professional growth of the pastor. What are the obligations of the pastor who is given a six- or nine- or twelve-month sabbatical leave? Is the pastor obligated to come back and serve the congregation for five more years to "repay" that leave? Is that a good idea? Or was the sabbatical fully earned when it was granted?

10. Who are the neighboring churches? What are they doing? What is the extent of interchurch cooperation with other parishes? Does the committee wish to encourage a greater degree of intercongregational cooperation in programming and ministry? Or does the committee place a higher priority on numerical growth? Frequently these are incompatible goals and the committee should be prepared to explain to the candidate which is a high priority and which is a low priority. The candidate should not accept "both" as an informed response. That usually represents an evasion of a hard question.

If the pulpit committee does not have this subject on its agenda, the prospective candidate should bring it up. In a few minutes much can be learned about the perspective of the pulpit committee by asking a few questions about what the other parishes in the area are doing and whether growth or cooperation is the higher priority.

One of the interesting recent products of the ecumenical movement is that occasionally a pulpit committee will invite the pastor of a nearby parish to serve as a nonvoting observer while they interview candidates. That can be remarkably beneficial for everyone involved.

11. One of the most vital issues in the life of nearly every congregation is the necessity of maintaining a sense of unity and common purpose among people who represent a wide range of views, and who come from widely differing backgrounds. The issue of unity in diversity should be on the common agenda. Which is given the higher priority by the various parties to the discussion, unity or diversity?

This tends to be a greater problem for the long established downtown church than for any other type parish because of the greater differences among the members in age, income, education, social and economic views, political affiliation, denominational background, racial, ethnic, or subcultural identification, definitions of the role or purpose of the downtown church, and length of membership. In most cities the downtown church either does include, *or has the potential for including,* in its constituency an extraordinarily wide range of people who together approach being a cross section of the community.

In some congregations the potential divisiveness of these differences is overcome by a strong doctrinal unity. In a few it is overcome by a remarkable sense of discipline, growing out of a strong commitment to Christ—although this is exceedingly rare in a large parish.

The most common approach to this problem is for the congregation to become a collection of groups rather than a collection of individuals. Each group must have a sense of its own identity and purpose and also must respect and tolerate the identity and purpose of the other groups. This concept of pluralism within the parish is a very important consideration when one discusses the future of any parish. Therefore, this entire issue should be on the agenda of both the pulpit committee and the prospective candidate. If this is a large membership church with a heavy emphasis on diversity, it is important that each of the larger constituencies within the congregation know that its perspective is represented by someone on the program staff. Which constituency has been left unrepresented by a departure that created a vacancy?

12. Closely related to this is the matter of visiting. Too many congregations are looking for a pastor with only two qualifications: competence as a preacher and a willingness to call in the home. While both are important, the pulpit committee of most parishes that have these two items at the very top of their lists probably is helping to destroy the parish it represents.

This is especially true of the parish with a thousand or more members. In a congregation of that size the issue of dealing with diversity will be a major challenge to the pastor. This and other responsibilities will leave little time for calling. An associate

will have to do most of the routine calling. A pastor of a
3,000-member parish in Texas responded to this subject by
describing his own role. He said, "When you are the pastor of a
congregation as big as this one, you're not a shepherd, you're a
rancher."

13. To be an effective pastor in the last years of the twentieth
century means hard work and lots of it! The minister should
have the emotional security, the administrative skill, and the
experience that makes it easy to delegate both responsibility
and authority. That, however, is not a substitute for productive
hard work! Most effective pastors share one common
characteristic; each is a remarkably hard worker.

There are major exceptions to this generalization. One is the
small and long-established parish; typically it averages sixty to a
hundred at worship on Sunday morning, and has a full-time
pastor. In many of these parishes the hardworking, hard-
driving, and efficient pastor can be a very destructive force.
That type of pastoral leadership can destroy both the parish and
the minister by trying to make what should be regarded as a
part-time job into a full-time vocation, by trying to make a
small congregation "perform" like the 600-member congregation served by a former seminary roommate, and by trying to
develop a response that quantitatively far exceeds the resources
available in that parish.

In these parishes the most effective pastors are usually those
who know how to channel their discretionary time left over
after "paying the rent"[3] into serving as a volunteer in
community, denominational, or interdenominational functions; or into golfing, fishing, and spending more time with the
family; or both.

The second exception is the very large congregation that
averages more than a thousand at Sunday morning worship. In
those congregations the ability to manage discretionary time
effectively, foresight, vision, the ability to conceptualize
abstract ideas, and a willingness to lead are far more important
than hard work.

14. The second most important characteristic that the pulpit
committee should be looking for as they seek a new pastor is a

candidate's attitude toward people. Does the candidate have a deep love for people? Is this minister sufficiently secure both emotionally and spiritually that competent and dedicated people are not perceived as threats? Does this concern for people come through? Do others find it easy to relate to this minister; to trust, confide in, and follow this leader?

In the past many churches have not placed much emphasis on this point in selecting a pastor. Frequently they sought a minister who could build and maintain the institution, and they called a minister who was object-oriented rather than person-centered in his or her world view.

Today and tomorrow the primary responsibility of the church will be ministry to people, both individually and in groups. Frequently this will be in a pastoral role to an individual or a family at a time of misfortune or disaster. At other times it will be in a prophetic role as a leader in an unpopular cause. Occasionally it will be in the minister's role as an enabler, helping others to discover and fulfill their ministry. Regularly it will be in a role as an administrator, as the pastor relates to both the paid staff and the volunteer leaders of the parish. In these and other roles the most important quality a minister can bring to his or her responsibilities is a genuine love for people that is experienced by the people, an interest in their problems, and a concern for them as God's children.

15. Finally, and while it is last, the most important of all the items on this common agenda is the question of whether the potential new minister feels the Lord is calling him or her to this church. To some this may seem so obvious that it barely rates mention. Experience, however, suggests this point cannot be overemphasized. Too often the pulpit committee concludes they have found the minister they have been seeking and begin to pressure the candidate to accept. Too often, however, it subsequently becomes apparent the candidate really was more interested in leaving an unhappy or uncomfortable pastorate, and the decision to move was more a desire to leave than a call to a new challenge.

While it is difficult, and perhaps pointless, to attempt to elaborate on this subject, let it be said simply that unless the pulpit committee believes the candidate "sees the vision," they should keep looking. If they extend a call, the candidate would be well advised to reject it unless he or she does "see the vision"!

Little or nothing has been said here about salary, housing, the prospective candidate's family, administrative ability, competence as a counsellor or fund raiser, or experience as a community leader. These omissions were deliberate, but should not be misconstrued as suggesting that they are unimportant considerations. This list was intended only to supplement the agendas of the two parties and to bring to their attention items one or both might overlook. It is not offered as a complete list, only as a supplement to the agenda of each party involved in the extremely important responsibility of picking a pastor for a particular parish.

There are a few subjects that some readers may feel are major omissions. These include the pastor's total compensation, the issue of a housing allowance versus a church-owned parsonage, the varying expectations on the new pastor's time and talent, the age of the prospective pastor, and the role of the pastor's spouse in the parish. Two of these are discussed in subsequent chapters.

Many congregations display great concern about the prospective pastor's spouse. They may be concerned over the spouse's education, employment, interest in functioning as an active leader in the congregation, talents as a gracious host or hostess, or role in denominational affairs. At best these are of second-level importance. The only two important questions for a congregation to raise about the prospective pastor's spouse are these: First, is the spouse happy that his or her mate is a pastor? If the spouse is unhappy with the mate's vocation as a pastor, this merits consideration. Second, is the spouse happy with the role as the spouse of a pastor and all that that may imply? This issue has grown in importance since 1965 with the sharp increase in the proportion of women among seminary graduates, and it can be expected to continue to be a significant factor as a growing proportion of the persons married to pastors pursue their own careers. (See chapter 16 for an elaboration of this subject.)

Back in the 1960s a joke in Presbyterian circles noted that at age forty-three a person was old enough to be elected President of the United States and young enough to be voted the most valuable player in the American Football League, but at forty-three a minister was too old to expect a call from a Presbyterian congregation. Those now ancient references to the careers of John F. Kennedy and George Blanda do contrast with the value systems of many parish leaders who voted for the former and applauded the last-minute heroics of the latter, but who also are convinced that "our next pastor should be under forty."

Rather than relying on chronological age, local church leaders might find it more helpful to ask another series of questions when interviewing a prospective pastor. Of more value than inquiring about age might be the answers to questions such as these: "What did you learn during the past year that will make you a more effective pastor this coming year?" "How do you believe your experience where you are now would be of help to you if you came here as the pastor of this congregation?" "What were the most helpful books that you read during the past year?" "What would you like to be doing ten years from now?" "What are your expectations for the future of the parish?" "How do you see the values of the generation of which you are a part influencing how you fulfill your ministry to the generation of people that constitutes a large part of our membership today?"

As parish leaders listen to the responses to these questions, they may conclude there is a vast difference between the person who has had fifteen years of experience and the individual who has had one year of experience fifteen times. That distinction may be a more useful index than chronological age in picking a new pastor.

M y wife, Mary, had just accepted what she thought would be a challenging half-time job in our local school system, teaching remedial reading, and we had absolutely no plans to move when the call came asking if we would be interested in going to St. John's," explained Donald Johnson, the thirty-seven-year-old minister at Trinity Church, who was in his fifth year as the pastor of that congregation.

"My first response was that I wasn't interested; but after we talked a little longer I finally agreed to meet with their committee next Thursday evening. Now that I have agreed to talk to them, I'm not sure what to say. Do you have any suggestions?"

There are at least five parts to an adequate answer to Pastor Johnson's question. Perhaps the best place to begin is with the first interview, which is the next item on his schedule. Some will argue that a better place for Don to begin would be to make absolutely sure his wife, Mary, is supportive of the possibility of moving.

When a pastor goes to meet with the pulpit or pastor-parish relations or screening committee from another parish, that minister immediately faces a very basic question. "Will I go with the expectation that the committee will interview me or with the expectation that I will interview the committee?" Or will this pastor-turned-candidate go without an agenda or plan, thinking of the meeting as a blank slate and hoping that someone will pick up the chalk and begin to write?

A pastor, such as Mr. Johnson, who was not planning on moving or who does not have to move, has a comparatively large degree of freedom in planning for the interview, but freedom does not grant the right to be irresponsible.

A reasonable expectation is that the pastor is entitled to one-half of that first evening to interview the committee. If the minister is prepared to assume the role of interviewer for an hour to an hour and a half, that can be a very effective way of making this a much more productive evening for both the committee and also the candidate.

It is not unusual for the committee to consist of from seven to twelve persons. Therefore, it is advantageous for all if the pastor asks permission to open the discussion with a few general questions. By doing this the candidate can ensure that every person present has at least two or three opportunities to speak early in the evening. This tends to encourage some who might otherwise be silent all evening to feel freer to speak. If the pastor encourages or allows the committee to ask questions for an hour or longer before raising any questions of the committee members, this may turn out to be encouraging a situation in which the candidate and the chairperson will do 70 percent of the talking. Chances are, the other 30 percent will be divided among four or five members of the committee, and the remaining committee members will be shut out of any active role in the discussion.

After the preliminaries have been completed, Mr. Johnson might say something like this: "I know you have many questions you want to ask me, but it might help me to respond to your questions more intelligently if you would permit me to ask a couple of questions first." If he receives a favorable signal he might follow with, "First, it certainly would help me if each one of you would tell me individually why you are a member of

St. John's Church. What were the circumstances, the event, the person, or the reason that account for your being a member of St. John's today rather than of some other congregation?"

With this question Don, in the space of ten or fifteen minutes, is able to (1) give every member of the committee a chance to be heard; (2) learn something about each committee member as a person; (3) identify both the timid and the bold persons on the committee; (4) discover a little about some of the major characteristics of St. John's; (5) determine the "mix" of the people that constitute the committee; (6) reveal to some degree how and why people join St. John's; and (7) help the committee members discover some things about each other and about St. John's that were unknown to some of them.

Following this initial round, Pastor Johnson may want to raise a second question to which each committee member again is asked to respond individually. The following questions have proved to be helpful in this process in other congregations. The prospective candidate may want to pick one or two from this list and adapt them, while others may prefer to develop their own questions.

"What is the most important strength or asset of St. John's as a church?"

"In terms of ministries or program, what do you folks at St. John's do best?"

"What new ministries or programs have been added recently or are under consideration?"

"What was the number one skill or gift or talent of your former minister?"

"If you could change one thing at St. John's, what would it be?"

"If you could wave a magic wand and have one wish about the life, program, and ministry of this parish come true, what would be your wish?"

"How will this congregation be substantially different from what it is today ten years hence? What changes will ten years bring to this church?"

"If you could change *one* thing in all that we do together as a denomination, what would you change?"

"If a twenty-nine-year-old teacher, his wife, and their two children, ages five and three, moved to your community from Seattle next month and visited St. John's on their own initiative, why might they decide to join? Why might they look elsewhere for a new church home?"

"If one of your members died and left St. John's $50,000 in her will with absolutely no restrictions on the use of the money, how do you think people would decide the money should be used?"

"What were the major goals that you as a congregation set for yourselves this year and how are you doing in reaching these?"

"When was St. John's at its peak in strength and vitality?"

"What is the most significant watershed in this congregation's history? Life here has never been the same since that event or date? What is it?"

Rarely will it be possible for the pastor to ask more than two or three of these subjective questions, but often asking even two of them not only will help free everyone to participate in the subsequent discussion, but also will elicit verbal and nonverbal responses that can be very enlightening to the candidate—and often to some of the committee members!

Why?

Sooner or later, if it appears that Don Johnson and the people from St. John's are interested in pursuing the conversations, the time will come when Don will want to review some of the statistical data about St. John's. How many people are members of this congregation? What is the average attendance at worship? How large is the church school? What were the total receipts last year?

A review of these data often can be more helpful if they are examined in a frame of reference consisting of these four elements.

1. What are the most useful statistics?
2. What are the trends over several years?

3. How do these figures compare with those of similar type congregations? -

4. If these numbers show significant changes from year to year, or contrast sharply with those of similar type congregations, why is this the case here at St. John's?

Perhaps the most significant single figure that can be used to describe a congregation to an outsider, and certainly the best single index to use in predicting other characteristics or trends, is the average attendance at worship on Sunday morning. There are a few congregations in which the qualifying phrase "on Sunday morning" will produce a distorted response because of the tradition of Friday evening or Saturday or Sunday afternoon or Sunday evening worship, or because of a recent shift to a major service of corporate worship on Thursday evening for those who will be away over the weekend. In perhaps 97 percent of the congregations in American Protestantism, however, the key index is still the number of people present for worship on Sunday morning.

This number can be compared to the communicant or confirmed membership figure, to the average worship attendance for the past several years, to the worship attendance of similar type and size congregations, and to the receipts from member giving.

It may be helpful to follow the Reverend Mr. Johnson as he reviewed the statistical data at St. John's and look at a few of the occasions when he felt constrained to ask the committee, Why?

St. John's reports a confirmed membership of 440, and that figure has hovered between 425 and 475 since seven years ago when it dropped from 583. Why?

"That really is deceptive change," replied one of the committee members very easily. "The year after Pastor Case came—he is the minister who is now leaving us for another pastorate—we decided to clean the rolls. The membership rolls had been neglected for years and it turned out we were paying denominational apportionments on 127 people who were dead, long gone from the community, or had simply lost interest in being a part of our church. I guess the previous pastor felt the denomination needed the money from these assessments or that it helped the prestige of the parish to report the larger figure."

For the previous six years the worship attendance at St. John's had averaged 226, 221, 219, 223, 213, and 199.

Why did it drop 10 percent in two years after being on a plateau for four years?

"Well, I'm not sure," replied the chairman of the committee from St. John's, "but Pastor Case explained that this decline was one of the reasons he felt that he should leave for another pastorate at this point in our history. Frankly, I for one agree it was time for him to move on. We had two major internal differences of opinion and a number of people had been offended. One was over the new plans for confirmation and the other, the music used in the worship service. Some feelings were hurt and little was done by anyone to be more considerate of the reactions of others!"

As he looked at these two sets of figures Pastor Johnson concluded that an attendance at worship equal to 40 to 50 percent of the membership was typical for a parish of this size and type in his denomination. If, however, this had been a denomination where that ratio is higher, such as the American Lutheran Church or the Christian Reformed Church, he would have persisted in his questioning. In the ALC, for example, a parish with a confirmed membership of 440 could be expected to average 250 to 300 at worship rather than 220.

The receipts for the previous year at St. John's had been $118,300, or an average of $600 per attender at worship. Since St. John's is a stable parish in a stable suburban community, Pastor Johnson had expected this figure to be approximately $600 times the average attendance at worship and therefore he said nothing about it. If this had been a small rural congregation, he would have expected the annual receipts to be $450 times the average attendance; if it had been a 1,200-member, downtown "First Church" type, he would have expected the giving level to be in the range of $1,000 to $1,400 per attender; while in the 1,900-member, metropolitan type church he would have expected it to be between $1,100 and $1,800.

When he saw that the total receipts for the past six years had gone from $76,400 to $89,600 to $101,300 to $115,900 to $119,800 to $118,300, he asked two questions.

"Why did the total receipts increase 50 percent in three years?" "Why did receipts level off during the past two years?"

Pastor Johnson next looked at what, in many congregations, is the third most useful statistical index: the number of persons who transferred their membership by letter into St. John's, minus the number who transferred out. He came out with this set of figures for the previous six years: 21, 19, 12, 2, -9, -27. With a trace of anxiety in his voice, he asked two questions.

"Why has there been this change from a net gain of 21 by transfer in to a net loss of 27 by transfer out?" "Why has there been a consistent downward curve year after year for six years?"

Don was especially concerned about this series of figures because he thought it might reflect the changing reactions of newcomers to the community and of visitors of St. John's to what they found or saw there. In responding to Don's first two questions on this subject the people from St. John's emphasized the mobility of people today, adding that in the past couple of years some unhappy members had transferred to other churches in the community. While he listened Pastor Johnson formulated another question on this subject.

"Am I hearing you say that six years ago newcomers to the community found St. John's to be an attractive parish when they went church shopping, but today, either they don't even shop St. John's, or if they do they decide to keep looking?"

Next Don noted that membership losses by death had been 9, 4, 8, 9, 8, and 10 for the past six years, or an average of 8 per year. In that denomination the annual death rate is 12 per 1,000 confirmed members. The rate at St. John's was an average of 18 per 1,000 members per year.

"Why," he asked the committee, "is the death rate so high in this twenty-two-year-old suburban parish? I would have guessed the death rate would be only about half of the denominational average, but here it is way above the denominational average."

"Well, it's true that this congregation is less than twenty-five years old," was the reply. "But, in case you didn't know, perhaps a fourth of our members are from the old St. Mark's Church, a congregation of older people in the inner city that merged with our church back in 1982. I suspect that that may be one reason for what you suggest is an unusually high death rate."

"I also have a question about the relationship between confirmations and deaths. You said earlier that at St. John's young people are received into confirmed membership when they are fourteen. Currently about 3.3 million people are celebrating their fourteenth birthday each year, and less than 2 million are dying each year in this country," continued Don, reviewing St. John's statistical record.

"Yet for the last six years you report 48 deaths and only 46 confirmations for all ages. I would have expected that in a suburban community such as this you would be averaging far more than twice as many confirmations each year as losses by death. Why is this total confirmation figure only 46 rather than somewhere in the neighborhood of 65 to 120 for these six years?"

"Please don't misunderstand the point of my questions," he added, when he suddenly realized that some members of the committee from St. John's felt that he was either criticizing or attacking them.

"We're here to talk about the possibility of my coming to serve as your pastor at St. John's. We met once and talked in generalities. You've heard me preach, and now we're meeting again to talk specifics," he continued. "I came to this meeting after doing my homework, and I simply am trying to learn more about this parish and what makes it tick. I'm not trying to be judgmental, I'm simply trying to learn enough so that I can ask the kind of questions that will help all of us come to the right decision."

Later that same evening they began to talk gingerly about
salary. The committee members were surprised to discover that
Don's cash salary as pastor of the 380-member Trinity
congregation was $21,000, or $2,600 above what St. John's had
been paying Pastor Case.

"We had been warned that when we went out to look for a
new pastor we would have to expect to pay close to $20,000,"
conceded the chairman of the committee from St. John's. "I
must confess I didn't realize that we were as far behind other
parishes in what we are paying as we seem to be. However,
don't worry about salary. We'll take care of you if we agree
you're the minister for St. John's."

"I'm not worried about what my salary might be if I come to
St. John's," quickly replied Pastor Johnson. "My question is,
Why did St. John's fall behind other comparable parishes in
what they have been paying in recent years? The six-year
record shows the cash salary went from $14,000 to $15,200 to
$16,800 to $17,500 to the current $18,400. Why has there been a
decline in the rate of the annual increase? That's the point that
interests me now!"

What's the Type?

In these negotiations with St. John's Church, Pastor Johnson
moved from the question of a strategy for that first interview to
a series of "why" type questions growing out of the statistical
data that had been made available to him.

A third area that merits exploration by the minister who is
contemplating a move to a new parish is the type or style of
parish under consideration.

In this case the move Pastor Johnson was contemplating
involved at least three types of change. The most obvious was a
change from the one-hundred-year-old, 380-member Trinity
Church, in a stable Iowa county seat community with 5,000
residents, to a younger and slightly larger congregation in a
growing suburban community in a metropolitan area with close
to a million residents.

Less obvious but equally significant would be the change in Pastor Johnson's personal and professional relationships as he moved from a rural to a highly urbanized community.

The most subtle change, however, would be in moving from a firmly established and stable county-seat-town type parish to a congregation that gave several signs of being in the process of changing from one type of parish to another.[1] The data that have been mentioned earlier suggest that St. John's may be experiencing what some church leaders describe as "a change of life." For more than a decade St. John's had resembled the typical young and growing suburban parish. When it passed the 500 mark in confirmed members, many people assumed that was but another milepost on a growth curve that would bring St. John's to the 1,000-member mark by its twenty-fifth birthday. Along about its fifteenth year, however, the growth curve began to level off, and St. John's, after a vigorous pruning of the membership roll, began to show signs that it was levelling off on a rather comfortable plateau. More recently it began to appear that this plateau was no longer level, but was beginning to tilt downward at the end exemplifying the future.

A few members of the committee felt uneasy about recent trends, and some of the questions Pastor Johnson had been asking had increased their uneasiness about the situation at St. John's. All the members were completely convinced, however, that everything would be all right again if only they could find the right pastor.

"I think I know the type of parish I am in back at Trinity," said Don in introducing his question, "but I am still uncertain what type of church you have at St. John's. I know Trinity, I know what it is, I know what is expected of me there, and I have a reasonable level of confidence that my gifts and skills are adequate for what is required of a pastor in that situation.

"I still don't know what type of church St. John's is," he continued. "I don't know what gifts and skills are required of a pastor in a parish such as St. John's is today or will be tomorrow, and therefore I honestly don't know whether I am the person you are looking for or not."

It would be unrealistic to expect the committee from St. John's to respond immediately with a thorough and analytical answer to a question such as Don had just asked. It also would be less than wise for Don to overlook the critical importance of this question. To move from Trinity to St. John's would be a far different change than to move from Trinity to a 700-member congregation in another midwestern county seat town.

What Are Your Expectations?

By opening up the question of the type of parish St. John's was, Pastor Johnson did accomplish two things. First, he helped everyone involved in the discussions, including himself, to begin to think about a question that often is overlooked, but frequently is of critical importance: matching ministers with congregations.

Second, he opened the door to the fourth part of the answer to his earlier question, when he had asked for suggestions of what he might talk about in his conversation with the people representing St. John's Church.

This has to do with expectations. What do the people at St. John's expect of their next pastor? of themselves? What can the next pastor expect of St. John's?

Most important of all, what do the people at St. John's understand to be God's expectations of them as a called-out community of believers in today's world?

As Pastor Johnson and the people from St. John's talked about what should be expected of the minister in a parish such as St. John's, it soon became apparent that each person held different expectations about the role of the next pastor and about the priorities on his gifts, skills, and time.

Thus before they finished discussing expectations they were already into the fifth part of the response to Don Johnson's earlier question about what a pastor should have on his agenda when contemplating a change in pastorates. It deals with pastoral priorities. While this subject belongs in this chapter, the process suggested for looking at this issue can be utilized in many other situations where a pastor and the people are struggling with the question of priorities. Therefore, this subject merits a separate chapter.

THREE

PASTORAL PRIORITIES

W hen it appeared that we might want to continue these discussions beyond the exploratory stage," commented the Reverend Mr. Donald Johnson to the 7-member committee representing St. John's Church, "I knew that sooner or later we would be getting into a discussion of the priorities on the time and energies of the person who becomes the next pastor at St. John's. So I sent off for a set of cards that are supposed to facilitate this process.

"Could we take a half hour and work our way through the process that is suggested here?"

"I don't see how it can do any harm," replied the chairman of the committee from St. John's, "and perhaps we'll even learn something."

"Here's a sheet of directions for everyone," continued Pastor Johnson, handing out the instruction sheets, "and here's a set of cards. Now let's walk through the instructions together before we go any further."

When they reached item 4 on the instruction sheet, they agreed that everyone would sort his or her cards on the basis of, What will have to be the priorities on the time of the new pastor at St. John's for the next year or two? Each person agreed that this was not a discussion of what the priorities would be under ideal conditions, but what the priorities should be in light of the existing situation.

It happened that as they gathered around a table the chairman was sitting to Pastor Johnson's left, so it was agreed that the rotation for each round would begin with the person sitting on Don's right. Thus the chairman would be the seventh person in the rotation and Don would be the last one to turn over his cards in each round.

After everyone had had ample time to study the twelve cards in the deck, discard the four lowest priorities, and arrange the remaining eight in order, face down on the table with the top priority card on the top of the deck, the man on Don's right was invited to turn over his top priority card and simply call out the name of the function or task.

"Visiting," said the first man.

"Teaching," called out the second member of the committee as she turned over her card.

"Enabler," announced the third.

"Leading worship and preaching," said a fourth, a woman in her mid-twenties.

"The leader," called out the fifth person in a very positive tone of voice.

"Leading worship and preaching," declared the sixth person in the rotation and one of the three women on the committee.

"Leading worship and preaching," said the chairman.

"Leading worship and preaching," said Don as he turned over his top card.

"Well, I see four of us are Christians," declared the sixth person in the rotation. "Leading worship and preaching is the basic reason a minister is set apart by ordination, and that should be the first priority on his or her time."

"I was reared in the Presbyterian Church," spoke up the middle-aged woman who was second in the sequence, "and there the minister is ordained as a teaching elder while the ruling elders are ordained from among the ranks of the laity in the congregation. I have always believed this was both symbolically and biblically the right way to do it. I think the first priority on a minister's time should be teaching responsibilities."

"Now, let's remember the ground rules," commented the man to Don's right. "We agreed that we would arrange these cards in the light of existing circumstances at St. John's, not in terms of how the world ought to be. Let's face it. The first priority on the new pastor's time at St. John's is to be a pastor to every member, and this means a lot of calling. At least a dozen families have said to me they feel St. John's has been without a pastor for at least five years."

"There's a lot of truth in what you say," agreed the fifth person in the rotation, "but I came out with a slightly different diagnosis. I think what St. John's needs is a pastor who is a real leader, a 'take charge' type of person. If we don't find that kind of minister, the downward curve at St. John's is going to get steeper!"

"Now you're raising a very basic issue," announced the third person to Don's right, "and that's the question of leadership style. What you're suggesting is a top priority on what is clearly becoming an obsolete style of ministerial leadership. We're not looking for a minister who will be *the* leader in St. John's. What we need is a person who sees the role of the pastor as being *one* of the leaders in the congregation. This means the top priority on the new pastor's time and talent is as an enabler. That's the style of leadership we need at St. John's today and tomorrow!"

"I categorically disagree with you on that," declared the middle-aged woman who was the second person in the rotation. "St. John's is too big to be led by a lay-clergy team. None of our volunteers has the time necessary to be part of an effective leadership team. That's been Pastor Case's approach and I'm convinced that it has been a big factor in why we haven't grown! Everyone in the church growth movement agrees growing churches have the benefit of strong ministerial leadership!"

"Perhaps it will help if we move on to the second card," suggested the chairman. "That should tell us whether we're as divided as we appear to be right now."

"Counselling," called the first man to Pastor Johnson's right, as he turned over his second card.

"The leader," said the woman who had placed teaching as the top priority.

"A leader among leaders," announced the man who had advocated enabler as the top priority.

"Evangelism," said the woman who was not only the youngest person in the group, but also the newest member of St. John's. Earlier she had placed leading worship and preaching at the top of her priorities.

"Administration," called out the man who had given top priority to the role of the pastor as *the* leader.

"Visiting," announced the sixth person, adding, as she nodded in the direction of the man to Don's right, "I'm with Jack over here; what St. John's needs is a pastor who can relate to the people on their own agenda. Our last minister was always so busy with his own agenda he never had time for anyone else's concerns. I put leading worship and preaching first, but among the choices we have here, visiting and counselling are going to be close seconds this first year or two."

"Administration," declared the chairman in a firm tone of voice as he turned over his second card. "A month ago I would have put teaching in second place, but after thinking about the questions Pastor Johnson has been asking us, I'm convinced that administration is second to leading worship and preaching. I'll bet that's what your second card says, too," he added as he turned to Pastor Johnson.

"No, I'm afraid not," replied Don as he turned over his next card and called out, "A leader among leaders."

"I think we need to stop and talk about that right now," interrupted the middle-aged woman who placed teaching first and the leader second. "If you mean you want to be part of a lay-clergy team, but won't initiate anything on your own, I can tell you right now that you've got at least one, and I expect two votes against you."

"At least two," agreed the fifth man in the rotation, who had placed a great emphasis on leadership in the first round.

"Let's hold off on that discussion for a few minutes," announced the man chairing the committee, "and finish the next six rounds. That will help us see both points of agreement as well as disagreement."

As the group continued with the next six rounds a three-way

split among the committee members from St. John's became increasingly apparent. Two were clearly placing the top priority on a pastoral role that would give the greatest emphasis to healing the wounds at St. John's. Two others were united around a high priority for the traditional functions of worship leader, teacher, and evangelist, while three made it clear that the most urgent need was for strong, aggressive leadership and administrative skills. This lack of agreement on the leadership role of the next minister subsequently emerged as a major issue that Don Johnson had to confront shortly after his arrival as Pastor Case's successor. That issue is discussed in more detail in chapters eight and nine.

When the group later examined the stack of discards, they found two additional interesting patterns. First, the discards contained eight "Denominational and Ecumenical Responsibilities" cards, seven "Community Leader" cards, six "Visiting" cards, and three "Evangelism" cards. In other words, there was a comparatively high degree of agreement that the first three of these functions of the ministry were very low on the priority list at St. John's. In this respect this was a representative group, since both laymen and pastors usually rank "Community Leader" and "Denominational and Ecumenical Responsibilities" very low.

The other pattern revealed by this examination of the discards was that "The Leader" card had been discarded by four persons, one of whom was Pastor Johnson. Four of the laity from St. John's had discarded "A Leader Among Leaders." This again is consistent with a general pattern, which finds that a majority of ministers support the "Enabler" and "A Leader Among Leaders" emphasis on leadership, while a majority of laymen tend to prefer a minister who is willing and able to be *the* leader in the parish.

There are at least four useful values in this process of determining the priorities people place on the various roles and responsibilities of a pastor.

The most obvious is that it gives everyone an equal vote. No one person can dominate the process of setting priorities. In a discussion format the individual who speaks most eloquently or has a very forceful personality often can sway some members of a group. In this process each participant has to do his or her own ordering of the priorities and then live with those decisions. As soon as every participant lays that stack of cards face down on the table, everyone gains a degree of invulnerability to being influenced by the priorities of others.

Closely related to this is the usefulness of this process in opening up differences in value systems that might otherwise be concealed by the rhetoric of a few and the silence of others. Once these differences are literally out on the table for all to see, they are easier to deal with.

A third value is that the process tends to make highly visible the very low priorities in the value systems of a majority, which never get attention because so often all the time is devoted to debating the top priorities.

Finally, this process tends to challenge the common assumption that "we're all in agreement on what we're looking for in a new pastor; our real job is then to find the minister who can meet our specifications."

This came through very clearly here in the work of the committee from St. John's Church. After they had finished examining all the cards, the chairman turned to Don and said, "Pastor Johnson, frankly I don't know whether you're the minister for us, or whether St. John's is the right parish for you. I do know, however, that you have done us two valuable favors tonight. The first was when you asked all those 'why' questions as you reviewed the statistical record from St. John's.

"The second was when you used these cards to help me see an important fact. I am not really the chairman of one committee, but the honcho of three small subcommittees—each with its own set of priorities—that have been masquerading as one committee. We really do not have a right to sit down and talk seriously with any minister about coming to St. John's until we complete our own homework and come to some agreement on what kind of minister we're really looking for. We're in your debt, sir, for helping us to see that we still have a lot of work to do."

With these comments the chairman highlighted a point that frequently is overlooked when a minister meets with a pulpit committee. Unless the candidate is so eager to find a new assignment that nothing can stand in the way of making a change, and thus is unwilling to accept this responsibility, the pastor being interviewed by a pulpit committee should try to help that committee as it carries out its responsibilities. It is reasonable to expect the minister being interviewed to help the pulpit committee improve its skills, its understanding of the task that has been assigned to it, and its capabilities to carry out that assignment in a responsible and effective manner.

The pastor who does move to a new parish probably will have many occasions in the years ahead to be grateful these inconsistent expectations were uncovered and that these sensitive subjects were discusssed back when the pastor was still seen as an "outsider." The candidate never will have that same degree of freedom after the call has been accepted or the appointment has been announced.

Even if the candidate does not move to the new parish, the time and effort spent in working with the committee to help them identify issues and to raise important questions may yield valuable benefits for a colleague in the ministry who does become the next pastor of that parish.

Postscript

The process for discussing and defining priorities that has been presented in this chapter was developed for use by pulpit committees and prospective pastors as they meet to discuss mutual expectations. It has been used widely for that purpose. The procedures and the categories suggested here represent the fifth revision in the development of the process.

Any layman or minister who would like to use this process is free to copy it as presented here. The right also is extended to adapt it by rephrasing or replacing some or all of the categories to fit more precisely the local circumstances. To be more directive, the reader is not only free to make such adjustments

What Are the Priorities?

What are the priorities on the minister's time in your congregation? What does the minister see as the order of priority on his or her time? What do the members believe it to be? One way to find the answers to these and related questions in your parish is to use a set of cards similar to those shown here. Here is a suggested procedure for using this process.

1. Reproduce enough copies so each member of the committee will have one sheet listing the priorities on the pastor's time in your parish.

2. Call together six to eight leaders in your congregation—the people who served on the pulpit committee when the present pastor was called, or on the pastor-parish relations committee or its equivalent.

3. Cut the sheet so each person has one set of cards; distribute these packs of cards to the people around a table.

4. Clarify the ground rules. Is the question, What *are* the priorities on the pastor's time in this congregation? or, What *should* be the priorities? or something else? Make sure everyone is responding to the same question.

5. Give everyone from five to ten minutes to look at the cards and sort them out, discarding what they believe to be the four *lowest* priorities on the pastor's time or the least important functions. *Without discussing what they are doing or the reasons for their choices*, each of them should arrange the remaining cards in the order of importance.

6. Begin with one of the laity and, moving in rotation around the table, ask each person to lay down his or her top priority card, face up on the table. While doing this, let each person state what he or she has chosen as the top priority and why. Continue around the table until everyone has placed their top priority card on the table. (It is often helpful if the minister is the last to lay down a card in this round.)

7. Discuss what the cards reveal. Are they all the same? Are there differences? If so, what do the differences suggest?

8. Continue the same pattern, with each person laying the second priority card just below the one placed on the table earlier. Discuss what the trend appears to be.

9. Continue with six more rounds.

10. Look at the four cards each person discarded earlier. Is there anything resembling a consensus in the discards?

Use this in any way you wish as a tool to stimulate creative and constructive discussion. Have fun!

THE LEADER	VISITING
Serving as *the* leader in the congregation—the person to whom members turn for advice and guidance on all aspects of the life and work of the congregation, and who initiates new ideas.	Calling in the homes of members or at their place of work in a systematic program to meet each member on his or her own turf.
COUNSELLING	LEADING WORSHIP AND PREACHING
Counselling with individuals on personal and spiritual problems, with couples planning to be married, with those who are hospitalized, with other people on personal and vocational problems, etc.	Planning and conducting worship services, including sermon preparation, and working with others who will participate in leading corporate worship.
COMMUNITY LEADER	ENABLER
Serving as a volunteer leader in the community to help make this a better world for all God's children.	Helping others identify their own special call to service and ministry and enabling them to respond to that call.
TEACHING	EVANGELISM
Teaching the confirmation class, planning or teaching classes for church school teachers or both, teaching in special short-term classes, teaching evening classes, etc.	Calling on the unchurched people in the community, bearing witness to the Good News, calling on prospective new members, and training the laity to be evangelists.
DENOMINATIONAL AND ECUMENICAL RESPONSIBILITIES	A LEADER AMONG LEADERS
Carrying a fair share of denominational responsibilities, participating in ecumenical groups and other cooperative bodies. Also, enlisting denominational and ecumenical resources for use in the local situation.	Serving with the lay leadership as one of a core of leaders in the congregation—each with his or her own unique gifts and each with his or her own special responsibilities—with the expectation this leadership team will initiate new ideas.
PERSONAL AND SPIRITUAL GROWTH	ADMINISTRATION
Developing and following a discipline of Bible and other devotional study, participating in programs of continuing education, and helping to plan and lead opportunities for personal and spiritual growth for others.	Serving as "executive secretary" of the congregation, working with committees, helping to plan the financial program of the church, working with committees on planning and implementing program, answering the mail, etc.

as are appropriate to the local circumstances, but is strongly urged to make them!

Another point at which this process can be helpful is at the time of the "review" meeting between the new pastor and several leaders from the congregation, usually scheduled approximately six months to a year after the new pastor arrives on the scene.

Pastor Johnson eventually did agree to go to St. John's. A week before he moved he wrote the chairman of the committee and asked that such a review meeting be scheduled for a specific time and place approximately six months later. In his letter he also listed six items that he wanted to be sure would be on the agenda for that meeting, and he urged the chairman to have his committee do likewise so that at least a major portion of what would be discussed would be defined early. Pastor Johnson felt that setting the date and formulating a specific agenda would reduce the chances for speculative comments such as these: "I hear the new pastor met with the pulpit committee last night. You don't suppose he is resigning already, do you?" "Now why in the world does he want to bring that up at this time?" "I wonder what she really means when she asks that question."

Among the six items Pastor Johnson wanted on the agenda were a discussion of his role as a community leader, an evaluation of his preaching, an evaluation of casual "drop-in" visiting, a review of the possibilities for in-service training opportunities for laymen, and a period of time for talking through the process of determining pastoral priorities, using a set of cards that would be especially tailored to the situation at St. John's.

It should not be assumed, however, that the process described here is limited to discussions between a pastor and a group of laypersons on the priorities on the minister's time and talents.

It can be and has been adapted to many other types of occasions when a group of people have to assign priorities among a range of demands. These include the priorities in the local church budget, the priorities among the goals of the

Christian education program, the expectations a United Methodist bishop has for the district superintendent, the priorities in the denominational budget, and the priorities on the time of the staff of a regional judicatory. In each case the basic values described earlier make this a useful procedure.

FOUR

THE
INTENTIONAL
INTERIM
PASTORATE

It was during the preliminary conversations with the representatives from St. John's that Pastor Johnson began to think about the alternatives open to him if he did move. One of the events that sparked his thinking was the conversation of several of his fellow pastors one night after the evening session at an overnight meeting of a denominational committee. As Don and a dozen other ministers sat in the dining hall drinking coffee about ten o'clock, one of the clergymen asked, "Does anyone else here know what it feels like to be an interim pastor?"

"The reason I ask," he continued, "is that I am just discovering this may be my own situation. A year and a half ago I came to Calvary to follow Dr. Henry Rogers, who had been the pastor there for nineteen years. I've about decided that my role is to serve as the transition between yesterday and tomorrow. For nineteen years that parish was built around the image of one man. Dr. Rogers was a strong leader, and the people simply followed his lead or got out. Anyone here know what I'm talking about?"

"I hear you, friend," spoke up another minister. "Some years ago I followed a man who had been the pastor of that congregation for twenty-eight years. I went there expecting that I, too, might stay twenty-eight years. I left after less than two years. After a few months I realized I had but two choices. I could try to follow in the steps of my predecessor and do things the way they had always been done, or I could break the mold, make a lot of people unhappy by encouraging new people to move into leadership roles, help introduce some new ideas, and then get out. I chose the latter. I left six years ago. A couple of months ago I got a tremendous letter of thanks from the minister who followed me. He wrote that he was just beginning to realize how I had helped make possible the wonderful ministry he is having there. He confirmed what I felt at the time, that that situation needed an interim pastor who would respond to the variety of feelings that surfaced with Dr. Rogers' departure, shake things up, open the doors to change, and then move on, carrying the hostility away with him."

"While my situation was different from what you two are talking about, I spent nineteen months as an interim pastor a few years ago," added another minister. "I followed a brilliant young minister who had died at thirty-three after a two-year, losing battle with cancer. His widow stayed in the community and taught school. The problem I had was that this man was 'present' far more than if he had moved to another parish. I dare say that during that first year two-thirds of the conversations in all the calls I made was about what a tragedy this was and how well the widow was adjusting. At least half the homes had his picture on the piano or the television set or the wall. For six months I was about the most frustrated preacher you ever saw. These people had canonized this fellow who had died prematurely, and I was trying to follow a god, not another mere mortal.

"After about six months," he continued, "I finally woke up to what was happening; so I deliberately spent the next year trying to help these people talk through their grief. I worked with the widow as she sought a place as a director of Christian education in a church in another state, and I did all I could to help that parish get ready for another pastor."

"What do you think should have happened in that situation?" inquired Don.

"This is only the seven-hundredth time I've thought about

that question," came the immediate response. "In my opinion, the leadership of the denomination should have encouraged that congregation to bring in an older minister—a retired pastor, for example—for ten months. He could have helped the people to work through their grief and to serve as a support group for this young widow. After several months he could have led them to begin to think about the future. As it was, I spent nineteen months doing accidentally—and probably rather clumsily—what could have been accomplished more effectively in one-half that time."

"You sound a little bitter," said one of the other men who had been listening in on the discussion.

"I don't think I'm bitter," came the reply, "but I know I'm smarter. We should all be more alert to these situations than we tend to be, and we should be more careful in what happens. For example, right now we have this huge supply of chaplains who have retired after twenty or thirty years in the military. We also have a lot of ministers who have retired from other kinds of chaplaincies who could have been asked to move into this situation and serve as a combination of pastor, father figure, and counsellor for a few months, until the people were ready to move on to the next chapter. Or, as another option, they would have benefitted from a year with a mature semi-retired pastor who didn't want a permanent pastorate."

"Maybe that's what should have been done in my last pastorate," said another of the group in a reflective tone. "I hadn't thought about it in these terms until tonight's discussion began, but I served a rather frustrating pastorate for four years before I moved to my present church.

"This may sound unbelievable," he continued, "but my predecessor in that church had come in September to follow a minister who had left his wife and run off with a member of the choir the previous June. Everyone was delighted when my predecessor arrived, because he had a lovely wife and two wonderful children, and was obviously a strong family man.

"By now you can guess what happened," he continued slowly to what was now a very attentive audience. "One night, fourteen months after this fellow's arrival, he disappeared with a married woman from the choir."

"What I want to know," interrupted one of the ministers, "is how come your wife agreed you should go to a church with that kind of choir?"

"By the time I got there things were in bad shape. A lot of people had quit the church, attendance was down to half what it had been three years earlier, the church was the butt of jokes all over town, and some people were talking about closing the doors," continued the former pastor of this demoralized congregation. "I have always been an activist, so I started right in to rebuild the program and get the people's attention off the past and on the future. I often said to my wife that our job was to replace gossip with the gospel, and backbiting with soulsearching. Along about the third year things began to move, but when the chance came to move from there to where we are now, I was glad to grab it.

"Now after hearing what you fellows have said, I'm beginning to get a new perspective on that situation. Maybe I was a four-year interim pastor in a situation that really needed about six months to a year with a solid, stable, mature minister who would help people talk through their problems and their distrust. Maybe if I had followed a short pastorate like that," he concluded reflectively, "I might have had a much more creative ministry in that situation."

As he listened to this conversation Don began to ask himself if he should ask the people from St. John's whether they were looking for an interim pastor or seeking a minister who would come with the expectation of staying for several years.

While this question actually had little relevance for the situation at St. John's Church, it can be a very relevant question. Whenever a change in pastors is under immediate consideration, all three parties to the new arrangement should ask themselves the question, Is this a situation in which it might be wise to consider an interim pastorate of from six to twenty-four months, to serve as a bridge between what was and what is to come?

The leaders in the parish should ask themselves this question.

The appropriate denominational executive should *always* pursue this issue when it appears to be a possibility. The prospective pastor should ask it before agreeing to move, especially if part of the attraction of the new position is the opportunity to leave an uncomfortable situation. Ignoring this possibility may mean the next move will be out of the pastoral ministry. Some of the most serious cases of professional disillusionment and personal frustration have resulted from a pastor's moving into what was believed to be a permanent pastorate, when the real need was for an intentional interim pastor.

There are at least six types of parish situations in which the concept of an intentional interim pastorate merits serious consideration.

The most common is that in which the pastor who has served a congregation for over fifteen years dies or retires. In approximately three out of four such parishes, regardless of whether the pastor dies or retires after fifteen or twenty or thirty or forty years, the next minister is an interim pastor. Not infrequently the new pastor does not recognize this, assumes this will be a normal pastorate, perhaps stays too long, does too little, and then leaves, a puzzled, wounded, and frustrated person. In perhaps one out of four of these long pastorates the way has been paved for the next pastor to come in and have a creative, fruitful, and rewarding pastorate. One example of this is when the people were ready, perhaps even eager for a change two or three years before the departure of that long tenure pastor.

The second type of parish where an intentional interim pastorate may be appropriate is closely related to the first. It is the church whose pastor, after fifteen or twenty years' service, moves on to another parish or to some nonparish position. The successor faces more favorable odds than the first type, but, in a majority of the cases studied, the next minister also is an interim pastor—though frequently that is not clearly perceived until many years later.

A third type frequently overlaps the first two, and can be seen most clearly in terms of leadership styles. The Christian churches in the United States, both Catholic and Protestant, have encouraged a strong authoritarian style of leadership. This style of leadership, and it is a style, not a leadership role, no longer is as popular as it once was, and sometimes is difficult to follow.[1] Among those who may encounter difficulties in following the highly authoritarian style of pastoral leadership are (a) the self-identified enabler, (b) the minister who prefers to react to the initiative of others rather than to lead, (c) those who see the pastor in a managerial role rather than in a leadership position, and (d) introverted ministers who also have a low level of self-esteem.

Many congregations have found that an intentional interim minister is a creative bridge between the departure of the highly authoritarian personality and the arrival of the next "permanent" pastor who may have a substantially different leadership style. Incidentally, such situations can usually be identified very easily by the procedure described in chapter 11. When this procedure reveals that the leaders ascribe 60 or 70 or 80 percent of the influence in the decision-making process to the senior minister, it may be time to consider an interim pastor for the transition period that will follow the departure of such a central figure.

A fourth type of situation in which an interim pastor may be appropriate was described earlier by the minister who had followed the thirty-three-year-old pastor who died of cancer. Whenever the termination of a pastorate is surrounded by considerable grief or turmoil, it usually is wise to bring in an intentional interim minister before considering the calling or appointment of a permanent pastor.

Another type can be placed under the general label of "major internal disturbances." One example of this was described by the pastor who had followed two ministers who had found the church choir an attractive recreational scene. Another is the parish that experiences a financial disaster. A third is the parish where the minister was charged with heresy and the trial dragged on for two years. Whenever the lay view of the integrity, status, or probity of the pastoral office has been undercut, consideration should be given to the restoration of the people's respect for that office before seeking a permanent successor.

A sixth type of situation in which an intentional interim pastorate may be the appropriate bridge between two eras is the parish that has been functioning in much the same way for decades, but now, it is clear to an increasing number of people, needs major changes. An example of this is the white congregation in a community into which an increasing number of blacks or Spanish-speaking persons are moving. Another is the parish that persists in perpetuating yesterday's patterns in the face of growing indifference, because "we have a good thing going—it's been working for years and we aren't going to take any risks by changing it." A third example of this type of situation is the small and long-established rural parish that finds itself surrounded by newcomers moving out from the city. Another example is old First Church downtown, which is faced with the choices of dying, relocating, or developing a new role for itself.

In each of these examples, an intentional interim pastorate of six months to two years may help bridge the transitional period. Ideally this will be a full-time, intentional interim pastor with a strong future orientation who also can serve as the resident planning consultant for that congregation.

While several persuasive arguments can be offered against this concept of an intentional interim pastorate, many of them overlook one of the central tenets of good parish administration. There are occasions when the "one thing at a time" agenda should be followed very carefully. Frequently the person who has the greatest freedom to ensure that first things are done first and the agenda is not overloaded is the minister who knows before arrival that this is a short term assignment as a transitional pastorate.

Perhaps the most widely asked question about this concept is, How can we prevent our new minister's tenure turning unnecessarily into an interim pastorate? The best response to that question is to suggest that both clergy and parish leaders recognize that some situations call for an intentional interim pastor and that others will turn into that type of situation if too much is expected of the new minister in the first several months in the parish.

A second question is, What can I do if I discover that I came thinking I would be the permanent pastor and I now discover the situation really calls for a short-term, intentional interim pastor?

One response is to redefine your role as the intentional interim minister, attempt to fulfill that role, and plan to move on after a year or two.

Another alternative, which has been implemented by several ministers, is to first accept and fulfill that unanticipated assignment as an interim minister and second, to consider the possibility of being your own successor. A senior minister of a large downtown congregation, who is in the eleventh year of what has turned out to be a happy, productive, and effective pastorate, did that. He spent a frustration-filled initial three years as the unintentional interim successor to a very popular eighteen-year pastorate and then succeeded himself. It can be done. Another minister followed a pastor who had been killed in a tragic automobile accident leaving a widow with two young children. The successor, who had been widowed fifteen years earlier, soon discovered she was an *unintentional* interim pastor, spent two years helping the members work through their grief, guilt, and sorrow and eventually was her own successor.

The only bad answer to the question is to pretend the need for an interim minister does not exist and to substitute the new pastor's agenda for the concerns and feelings of the people.

Perhaps the most critical question that occasionally arises is, If I accept a position as an intentional interim pastor, should I make myself available to become the permanent pastor? Nearly everyone who has worked with this concept agrees the answer to that question is an emphatic, no!

An increasing number of mature ministers are raising questions about interim pastorships and where training is offered. The Christian Church (Disciples of Christ) probably has accumulated more experience with this concept than any other denomination, with the Episcopal Church a close second.

The Missouri Region of the Christian Church (Disciples of Christ) in the early 1980s came as close to perfecting the concept as any regional judicatory has been able to do. The Alban Institute and the Mid-Atlantic Association for Training and Consulting in Washington, D.C., offer resources and training opportunities for prospective interim pastors. The demand is growing and the responses to that demand are becoming increasingly sophisticated.

FIVE

THE
PASTOR'S
COMPENSATION

Recently two Presbyterian ministers returned home after a short trip out of town. As the first one walked into his home he received an enthusiastic welcome from his wife, who reported joyfully, "There's a letter for you from St. Andrew's Church." On opening the envelope the minister found an invitation from the chairman of the pulpit committee of that congregation to come for a second interview to discuss the terms of a possible call.

With both hope and fear in her voice his wife urged, "You're going to go, aren't you? If they extend a call, we can move out of this dump and get into a decent manse that has enough room for our family."

Four or five hours after the second minister arrived home his wife casually mentioned to him, "Oh, I guess I forgot to lay it out, but there's a letter for you from Westminster Church. I wouldn't be surprised if they're asking you to come back and meet with their pulpit committee again. I don't know why they're so persistent. They saw this house, and I can't understand why they would expect us to want to move out of this new home into that hundred-year-old shack they call a manse at Westminster!"

These two illustrations lift up one of the most neglected factors, which also is often an extremely crucial element in the

65

"compensation package" received by the effective pastor—a happy spouse. (This brief discussion will focus on the lay woman married to an ordained husband. Clergy couples and the lay man married to an ordained wife, while both represent growing segments of the population, constitute two substantially different sets of concerns.)

The congregation can contribute to the pastor's wife's happiness in many ways, including such variables as viewing her as another member of the congregation rather than as a supply of free clerical labor and allowing her the same freedom to say no that is granted other members. Another contribution to the personal well-being of the minister's wife is providing a good residence for the minister and his family. The minister's spouse who is happy in her role as the wife of a clergyman can be a major asset to his ministry. The wife who is unhappy with her role or discontented with the housing can be an inhibiting factor in her husband's ministry.

As the representatives from St. John's Church talked among themselves, they decided they would offer Pastor Johnson and his wife their choice of a housing allowance or the use of the church-owned parsonage.

"Let's give them a choice and let them make the decision," advocated Jack Peterson. "In the meantime we can concentrate on such questions as salary, car allowance, and other items."

"I had a chance to talk about pastors' salaries with Paul Peters from the denominational office the other day," added Everett Wright, "and I think we should work up a list of items so we don't forget anything. I'm convinced that Pastor Johnson is the minister we're looking for, and I don't want any neglected little detail breaking up what looks to me to be a promising relationship. I believe in getting every question settled in advance so there won't be any misunderstandings later on."

"I'll second that," said Betty White. "Let's start making out our list."

After meeting among themselves for two evenings, the committee from St. John's agreed on the following list, as they prepared for what they hoped would be their final meeting to complete the arrangements with Pastor Johnson.

1. Cash salary—An annual rate of $22,500 per year for the balance of this calendar year and a $300 increase effective the first of next year.

2. Car allowance—$300 per month, based on the assumption that the pastor at St. John's would have to travel 18,000 miles a year on church business.

3. Insurance—The parish to pay both the parish's and the pastor's share of the denominational health, accident, and liability insurance program for ministers.

4. Pension—The parish to pay the whole 14 percent of the pastor's salary required by the denominational pension program.

5. Book and periodical allowance—The parish to pay up to $250 for subscriptions to professional and religious periodicals and for books.

6. Continuing education—In accordance with the denominational plan, the parish to "deposit" two weeks' time and $300 in cash each year in a continuing education "bank." Pastor Johnson could "spend" this each year or allow it to accumulate; for example, at the end of four years he could "withdraw" eight weeks of educational leave time and $1200. The denomination was prepared to match the parish dollar for dollar up to $200 per year, and the minister, as a professional, was expected to pay part of the total cost.

7. Vacation—Two weeks for the balance of this year, three weeks next year, and four weeks each year beginning with the second full year.

8. Housing—A choice of $9,600 per year in a housing allowance *or* use of the church-owned parsonage with the parish paying for all utilities and maintenance.

9. Moving expenses—St. John's to pay the cost of moving expenses up to a maximum of $1600.

10. Sick leave—The pastor to be granted one day of sick leave each month, and this to be accumulated up to a total of 120 days. In order to discourage casual use of sick leave the parish to make a payment of one month's salary for each two months of unused sick leave when the pastoral relationship is terminated.

As they looked over the list, near the end of the second evening, Jack Peterson commented, "I feel kind of like a fool, walking into a meeting with a minister and laying a list such as this on the table. I'm especially embarrassed by the items on vacation, moving expenses, and sick leave. This list makes it look like we think we're some big corporation, and not just a friendly little church. I still think we ought to say simply that we'll pay his moving expenses, whatever they turn out to be, give him three or four weeks' vacation every year, and, if he gets sick, we'll take care of him. We're looking for a pastor, not an executive."

"I'm willing to discuss any changes you want to suggest," replied Everett Wright, who had been the leader in drafting the list, "but I'm firmly convinced that the fairest way to begin an arrangement with a new pastor is to do everything we possibly can to prevent any future misunderstandings. After fifteen years as a personnel officer I'm convinced the best way to do that is to try to foresee as many contingencies as possible and at least to arrive at a tentative agreement. I think it best to be as businesslike as possible in these matters."

"I kind of agree with Jack," interjected Betty White, "but I believe everything on our list belongs there. It does look terribly impersonal, though. Maybe what we should do is call Pastor Johnson, tell him we're coming to next week's meeting with a list of items to be discussed, and urge him to bring his own list. Maybe that way we'll not look so businesslike, and we'll also get some ideas from him."[1]

The committee agreed to follow Mrs. White's suggestion, and the chairman telephoned Don and asked him to come prepared with his list.

To say the committee was a little startled when they compared Pastor Johnson's list with their own is something of an understatement! To begin with, they had felt somewhat guilty about bringing a list with ten items on it. Pastor Johnson's list had twice as many:

1. An agreement that this committee or an appropriate successor group to be named by the church council will meet with the pastor for two hours six months after his arrival at St.

John's, to discuss (a) the congregation's expectations of him and his performance and (b) his expectations of St. John's.

2. An agreement that such a review committee will meet with him every six months thereafter.

3. St. John's will provide a full-time church secretary on a forty-hour-a-week basis, to replace the present arrangement of twenty-five hours a week and an occasional volunteer.

4. The pastor will be encouraged to spend four days a year visiting other congregations to see what they are doing and to learn what he can to help him in his ministry at St. John's.

5. At least two laymen will accompany him on two days of these visits every year.

6. The church council will agree to an overnight, Friday-evening-and-all-day-Saturday planning retreat at least once a year, preferably to be scheduled one or two months after the seating of the new members of the church council, who are elected at the annual meeting in January.

7. At least one-half of the church council will participate in some kind of in-service training program for laymen every year.

8. The parish will include at least $800 in the budget each year to pay for lay training events.

9. The pastor's wife will be expected to be a member of St. John's parish, no more, no less.

10. For every call the pastor makes on members *or* nonmembers, laymen from the congregation will make at least one call.

11. There will be an annual accounting of these calls to the parish by *both* the pastors and the lay callers.

12. The parish will participate in the denominational program for the continuing education of pastors. (This was the same as the committee's item 6.)

13. The parish will pay all utilities at the parsonage.

14. The beginning salary will be $22,500 per year.

15. St. John's will pay twenty-two cents a mile for church-related travel.

16. St. John's will pay the monthly cost of the denominational pension program.

17. St. John's will pay the full premiums in the denominational health insurance program.

18. St. John's will pay all expenses of this move.

19. Vacation time will be three weeks per year, *in addition* to time for continuing education events and for Don's obligations as a counsellor at summer church camp.

20. St. John's will agree to pay the parish's share of the cost for Don to spend three days in the denominational career counselling center after he has had five years of service at St. John's.

As she compared these two lists Betty White exclaimed, "I was afraid I would be embarrassed by our being too businesslike and precise in our list, but your list really is far more comprehensive and specific than ours. I guess I'm embarrassed at how much emphasis we placed on economic considerations, while your list is dominated by concerns about ministry and what you expect of us."

"Please don't feel embarrassed," replied Pastor Johnson. "When you asked me to make up a list, I started to think in terms of salary, pension, insurance, and vacation. Then it occurred to me that here was a unique opportunity to discuss about what I'm really concerned about in terms of compensation. My list really breaks down into three parts. The first deals with what I call satisfactions. Several items, such as 1, 2, 11, and 20, fit into that category. I want to know how I am doing in my job, and also receive some honest evaluations of my work. Overlapping that first category are my concerns for strengthening the lay ministry of the church. I've mentioned these before. I decided we would understand each other better if you could see what my expectations are of the people at St. John's.

"Finally," concluded Pastor Johnson, "I thought I should include what I expected you would want me to put on my list when we talk about compensation."

As they discussed the two dozen items on the two lists, the members from St. John's and Pastor Johnson agreed that he was the minister they were seeking and that this was the place for his next pastorate, as well as agreeing on his compensation. Perhaps more important, however, was the fact that they also came to a better understanding of of each other's expectations than they might have achieved had they come together simply to discuss salary.

SIX

WHAT DO
YOU PAY
THE LAITY?

W hat do you pay your Sunday school teachers?"
When Pastor Johnson asked this question of a
member of the Christian Education Committee at St.
John's Church the second week after his arrival, the response
was a series of puzzled frowns.

"I suppose there are some congregations that pay their
teachers," finally commented Mrs. Boden, "and I suppose it's
all right, if that's what they have to do to get enough teachers,
but here we've always relied on volunteers. We don't have the
money to pay them even if we wanted to, and I don't think we
either want to or should pay them."

"When I think of the difficulty we have had in getting
volunteers the last few years," added the chairman, "we may
have to begin thinking about paying them. Right now we have
three teachers who have announced they won't be able to
continue in the fall, and there isn't a volunteer replacement in
sight."

"If they took their vows as church members seriously,"
spoke up a grim-faced Mr. Brant, "they should volunteer to
work where they're needed in the church and not expect to be
paid. That's part of what's wrong with the country today,
nobody wants to do anything unless they're paid for it."

This discussion missed the point of Pastor Johnson's original question. Every church pays its volunteers; the question is, What does it pay them?

The compensation for volunteer service takes many forms. These include the feeling of satisfaction that often accompanies a positive response to a real need, a sense of personal fulfillment, satisfaction with a job well done, "repayment" for services received from others, reinforcement of a sense of personal worth or value, a response to the obligations incurred by membership in an organization, "brownie points," a channel for expressing neighbor-centered love, prestige, status, public recognition, earning a sense of belonging in that organization (for many new members of any voluntary association, the most effective channel for assimilation is by works or volunteer service), anticipation of rewards in heaven, "evening the score," fellowship, and the opportunity for personal growth, development, faithfulness, and learning a new skill.

A seventy-three-year-old retired farmer, who lives in a town in Nebraska, two or three times a week drives out to the country to help his son with the farm work because "there really is too much for one man to do by himself." This retired farmer's greatest satisfactions come every spring, when he can go out with a huge disk-harrow and, in one day, prepare forty or fifty acres for planting. He often contrasts this "good day's work" with what he could accomplish fifty years ago, when he was in his physical prime. In the 1930s in a good day, using a walking plow, he could just begin the preparation of two acres of land for the spring planting. What does his son pay him? Nothing in cash, but a tremendous amount in what the behavioral scientists identify as "psychic rewards."

The importance of psychic rewards or "satisfactions" often is overlooked as the leaders in the local church plan the allocation of volunteer manpower. At least five dimensions to this issue merit the concern of both the pastor and the people in every congregation. One of these can be illustrated by returning to the conversation at St. John's that was reported in the opening paragraphs of this chapter.

After it was explained that the question included non-financial payments to volunteers, one member added in a very positive voice, "I believe the greatest reward or compensation we could offer a Sunday school teacher would be the guarantee that every Sunday morning he or she will be able to walk into the classroom and find a group of well-behaved and quiet youngsters waiting for the presentation."

As soon as the three teachers on the committee recovered from their laughter, one of them responded, "I'm afraid you're dreaming of another planet, Mary. We're not expecting to find a roomful of little angels sitting there when we volunteer to be teachers. What we would appreciate, however, would be reasonable working conditions, relevant materials, interesting resources, decent training opportunities, and some counselling help when difficulties arise."

This teacher was lifting up a basic point in her response. The psychic rewards offered volunteers have to be (a) realistic and (b) meaningful or rewarding to the recipient *from the perspective of his or her own self-perceived needs.*

Another dimension of this issue might be labelled The Golden Rule of Rewarding Volunteers, or "do not return bad for good."

One of the most widespread examples of this is the compensation plan used by many congregations in rewarding persons who volunteer to go out calling. For example, at St. John's Church the practice for several years had been to ask each individual or family to bring to church on Loyalty Sunday the card on which they had recorded their pledge toward the church budget for the coming year. Typically this brought in cards from 70 percent of the households in the parish, some of which were mailed in during the days just before and after Loyalty Sunday.

The finance committee distributed the names of the families from whom no pledge card had been received among fifteen volunteer callers. Each volunteer received five or six cards with instructions for calling at these households and asking for a pledge to the church budget.

While it was not done consciously or deliberately, what had been happening at St. John's was that most of the calls that would have been pleasant, satisfying, and rewarding for these volunteers had been taken care of by the Loyalty Sunday approach. Most of those who would offer an affirmative response when approached had either brought in or mailed their pledge cards. Consequently, four out of five calls made by the volunteers were to persons who were neutral or unhappy in their feelings toward St. John's. If they did sign a pledge card, the decision to do so often was motivated by guilt, by the hard-sell approach of the caller, or by the conclusion that the easiest way to terminate this visit was to sign a pledge card.

There are few satisfactions for the caller in this kind of approach. Had St. John's been more conscious of the compensation it was providing for its volunteer callers, it would have used an every-member visitation system. This usually produces a sense of satisfaction and accomplishment for the caller in three or four out of every five calls. Also this plan usually has the fringe benefit of producing from 5 to 15 percent more money in pledges than the approach St. John's was using.

The same pattern of building in a high level of frustration and dissatisfaction for the volunteers can be found in calling programs directed at members who have not attended worship during the past year, people who are behind schedule in paying the amount they pledged to the church, or people who are not members of the church yet who are being asked to contribute time and material toward the annual money-raising event at the church.

A far better method of building higher levels of satisfaction for the caller is to concentrate on calling programs in which the agenda for the call is meeting the needs of the person being called on rather than "pushing our product." This type of calling effort also is far more effective in helping the church identify and respond to the needs of people.

A third way in which many churches reward their volunteers was reflected by the comment of the ex-board member who

explained, "When I was on the official board, I knew
everything that was going on around here. Now that I've been
off the board for two years, I'm not as well informed about
what's going on." In that church, as in many other
congregations, a careful and consistent effort is made to make
sure that at nearly every gathering of volunteers some time is
devoted to sharing information. For many people the
satisfaction of being very well informed members is an
important part of the reward system for volunteers.

A fourth aspect of the issue of rewards for volunteers was
introduced by the teacher who spoke of her desire for training
opportunities.

Pastor Johnson had placed this item on the agenda for the
review session scheduled for six months after his arrival at St.
John's, but, when the subject came up earlier, he did not
hesitate to follow up on the opportunity.

"If we think of the feeling of satisfaction that accompanies
the completion of a job that has been done well as an important
payment for volunteers," he suggested, "perhaps we should
place a greater emphasis on the training that enables a person to
carry out the task for which they have volunteered."

"That sounds great, but we have tried training programs
before, and it's like pulling teeth to get the people who need the
training to attend," responded the chairman.

"That's a very widespread problem," agreed Pastor Johnson, "and we'll have to give this some careful consideration, but
I am convinced that if we can provide training opportunities in
those areas where our leaders and teachers feel they need help,
we'll get a response. Too many training programs are
developed around what the persons planning the training
program *believe* the people need, rather than in response to the
real needs of the participants. On the other hand, we all
recognize it is impossible to teach an adult anything that he or
she does not want to learn."

Pastor Johnson was correctly identifying one of the critical
items in the reward system for volunteers, training opportunities designed to meet the felt needs of the people involved in the

training ventures. Churches are notorious for assuming that simply giving a person a title carries with it all the skills necessary to fulfill the responsibilities that accompany the title. This pattern is similar to paying a person with a check that looks very impressive until it is taken to the bank and found to be worthless.

Later that same evening Pastor Johnson brought up a fifth facet of this issue when he asked, "What is the procedure for recognizing the contributions of volunteer leadership?"

"Well, we have a commitment service every September for the church school teachers and officers," replied Mrs. Boden. "Is that what you mean?"

"No, I'm thinking of some means of saying thank you to those who have served during the year. What do you do to lift up what has been accomplished and to thank those who have helped make these accomplishments possible?"

"Three or four years ago we tried something like what I believe you're suggesting," replied Mr. Brant, "but it didn't work out very well. We had a big banquet here at the church to honor all the volunteers. I was one of the trustees, and we paid for it out of our own pockets; it didn't cost the church a dime. Eight of us chipped in fifty dollars apiece to pay for a catered meal. It was really a flop, though, and I don't think anyone wants to try that again.

"You see, Reverend," he continued as he addressed the new pastor, "the people here at St. John's really fall into two categories. There's a small group of us who take our church vows seriously and do our jobs because we love the Lord. We don't expect or want or need any special thanks or bouquets. The rest of the people here want to get by as cheaply as they can. They want to do as little as possible—and that includes staying away from a banquet to honor those who do carry the load here."

"I think I hear what you're saying," replied Pastor Johnson, with complete honesty, "and I guess we should postpone any more discussion on this or we won't get through the rest of the agenda."

As he walked down the street from the church to the parsonage later that evening, Pastor Johnson, who believes very strongly in an "affirm and build" style of pastoral leadership, had a strong hunch that he was on the trail of a potential "winner" in this new pastorate.

SEVEN

WINNERS
AND LOSERS

P reacher, I want you to know that, for the first time in my life, world missions has my attention," said the sixty-one-year-old president of the First National Bank, as he wrote out his personal check for $10,000.

As he repeated this comment from one of the parishioners at First Presbyterian, Dr. Frank Harris added, "And that is one part of the story of how we increased our special offering for world missions from $4,200 to $40,000 in one year."

This conversation really had its beginning a few months after Don Johnson came to the pastorate of St. John's Church. He had accumulated since his arrival nearly a dozen items for his "worry list."

This list included a disproportionately low percentage of the total receipts being allocated to the ministry to others; a record of attendance at church council meetings that had averaged between 40 and 60 percent for the past several years; a continuing decline in church school attendance; the experiences with two newcomer families, who joined other churches after they had visited St. John's and found it, in their words, "cold" and "unfriendly"; a real question of whether St. John's should continue the advertisement for the church on the Saturday religion page of the metropolitan newspapers; the levelling off in worship attendance; the clearly apparent decline in the women's organization; the dull youth fellowship; the lack of growth in parish membership in a situation in which all outward signs suggested the parish should be continuing to grow in size and vigor; and the lack of imagination among some of the key leaders.

While he had a few ideas of his own about what needed to be done, Pastor Johnson had decided he would use part of the "honeymoon" while he was new at St. John's to go out and get acquainted with other pastors in the area and see what they were doing that might help him be more effective at St. John's. Therefore, in each conversation with another pastor he injected a question such as, What's happening here that's exciting? or, What happened in this parish that has stirred up the people here? or, What are you doing here that might be of interest to an outsider?

When he went to see Frank Harris at the First Presbyterian Church, he was impressed to learn that this congregation had increased its extra giving to world missions tenfold in one year. He immediately asked, "How?"

"Last year we only raised $4,200 for world missions over and above our regular benevolence budget," replied Dr. Harris. "Some of us thought that was pretty bad for a 2,700-member congregation, an average of less than two dollars a member for our special offering for world missions.

"We decided that it was our fault, that our committee had not done enough to dramatize the need, and that we shouldn't blame our people for being cheap. So we decided we would symbolize the whole effort by one part of our special appeal, which was to buy a tractor for one of the new African nations. We borrowed a $24,000 tractor from a dealer here in town and parked it in front of our church one Sunday morning. For some reason or other it didn't get moved for a few days, and one morning a banker came storming in and wanted to know why the custodian was leaving our tractor out in the open, and especially why he had left it in front of the church where it was in people's way when they wanted to get into the building. I suggested that instead of jumping on me he talk to Angus

McPherson, who is chairman of our building and grounds committee.

"A day or two later he came back and said, 'Preacher, you knew all along why that tractor was out there. You just set me up when you sent me to see Angus.' I told him I had thought Angus would be able to explain it better than I could," continued Frank Harris.

"Well, to make a long story short, Angus explained to him that as ruling elder he should know (a) this congregation didn't own a big tractor like that one; (b) the tractor symbolized the special appeal for world missions; and (c) the church was dependent on people like him to make sure this special appeal raised a significant amount of money. So the banker said to me, 'Preacher, what do you think I should be doing about this appeal?' I told him our goal was $40,000 and that one man had offered to contribute fifty cents for every dollar the rest of the congregation contributed. I suggested that if he was serious in asking what he could do, he could match the offer of this individual and the two of them together would match the rest of the congregation dollar for dollar. He agreed to do this, and I am firmly convinced that when he wrote out that check for $10,000 he had a greater interest in world missions than he had ever had before."

"Now are you suggesting that this idea of getting a couple of people to match the rest of the congregation on a dollar for a dollar basis is the best way to raise money for world missions?" asked Don Johnson in a somewhat puzzled voice.

"You missed the two key points of my illustration," replied Frank Harris. "What I was trying to emphasize was the importance of a goal and of helping people see where the money is going. A year ago we simply passed out the special offering envelopes and asked people to give whatever they thought appropriate. This year we set a high goal, *and we had the tractor out there so people could see how part of the money would be used.*

"Furthermore, and I don't think we should overlook this, when our friend wrote out a check for $10,000 for world missions, it motivated him to want to learn a lot more about what the church is doing in world missions. If we had simply permitted him to stick a $10 bill in an envelope some Sunday morning we would have denied him the chance to have his curiosity aroused about what happens to the money. I firmly believe that a man who can write out a check for $10,000 for world missions *should* be curious about what the church is doing and how the money is being used," concluded Dr. Harris.

"What will you do next year?" inquired Don Johnson, in a voice that suggested he was asking, How are you going to top this?

"We're working on that now," replied the Presbyterian pastor. "We have four task forces, each composed of six people. One task force will visit Presbyterian work in South America, another, the work in Africa, another, in the Far East, and the fourth will visit some of the mission work here in the United States. Those twenty-four people will compose half of a 48-member committee that will recommend to the Session our goal for next year for the special world mission offering. We have $300,000 for the benevolences in our regular budget of $1.2 million. In addition, this year we will have special offerings of at least $200,000 for benevolences over and above the budget. That means that out of total receipts of $1.4 million approximately a half million will go for benevolences."

"At St. John's they have had a unified budget for years and everything for benevolences is in the regular budget," commented Pastor Johnson. "You're telling me, if I hear you right, that you have both a unified budget *and* special offerings?"

"That's right!" replied Dr. Harris. "Our goal here is to use 40 percent of our total receipts for benevolences and 60 percent for local expenses—and I expect we'll reach that goal in another year or two. Next year we'll be up to about 36 percent."

"Couldn't you do it with a unified budget?" asked Don.

"Nope, the unified budget's a loser on that point. The floor becomes a ceiling," replied the Presbyterian pastor firmly. "It may sound like a great administrative idea, but if you're interested in helping the people understand what is happening, how the money is being used, and how they can help as the church responds to the needs of people, the unified budget is a loser and the special offering for designated causes is a winner. Now please don't misunderstand me, I am strongly in favor of building into the regular church budget the denominational asking for benevolences. I'm talking about going beyond simply 'paying our denominational dues.' The unified budget is both a floor and a ceiling on benevolence giving. If we tried to get up to 40 percent of our unified budget for missions, the only way we could do that would be to squeeze out what I believe are essential programs for our members. We allocate a fourth of our unified budget for benevolences. Anything above that would hurt our local ministry. The only way we can reach our 60-40 goal is by special appeals."

"But I've always been taught that people don't like to be bothered with special appeals every month or two," objected Don.

"You've been listening to too many preachers," replied Frank Harris. "The *North American Interchurch Study*[1] made it very clear to me that the level of giving is greatly influenced by how clearly the people understand the need. A unified budget tends to conceal needs while a dozen carefully publicized special offerings each year help people see the needs more clearly. We can't expect every member to give to every special appeal, but when we have about a dozen, we are pretty sure we'll offer most of our members one or two opportunities that will coincide with their special concerns. We could never expect to reach our 60-40 division between local expenses and benevolences without the advantages of special opportunities for designated giving.

"Let me give you one more example," continued Dr. Harris. "Last spring we decided we needed to take up an extra special offering for world hunger because of the famine in Africa. If we had simply announced it one Sunday and received the special offering the following Sunday, I expect we would have raised about $4,000 to $6,000. Instead of that, we appointed a special ad hoc committee to study the situation and recommend a goal. They recommended a goal of $50,000, the Session approved it, and that total offering came to about $55,000. That illustrates my basic point again. People do believe in the basic Christian principle of stewardship, but in this day when they are being bombarded with so many requests for money, their natural tendency is to give a token amount unless they are challenged with a clearly defined goal to meet a highly visible need."

"Well, thanks for your time," responded Don Johnson gratefully as he stood up to leave. "I think I have several ideas on how to turn a loser into a winner at St. John's."

Later that same morning Don dropped by to see Charlie Williams, who was the pastor of a Presbyterian church in the next municipality. Mr. Williams was arranging a display of color photographs in the church parlor.

"What are you up to today?" inquired Don as he walked in on his perspiring friend.

"Getting ready for the Session meeting tonight," came the reply. "Soon after I came here a year ago I suggested that we meet in here instead of in the fellowship hall in the basement. There the Session members sat on folding chairs around tables and had a dull, dry, and staid business meeting every month. About a third of the Session members stayed away from it with regularity. When we moved up here, where we sit in comfortable chairs in an attractive setting, our average attendance for a Session meeting jumped from eighteen to thirty-two. That's pretty good considering there are only thirty-six members of the Session! So I decided that I should reciprocate by having a different display each month showing what we're doing as a congregation. This month I'm using a bunch of pictures showing what's happening in the Interfaith Housing Park this congregation helped to sponsor."

As he drove home that morning, Don decided he would suggest that St. John's move its monthly meeting of the church council from that barren basement classroom into the church parlor.

A couple of weeks later at the monthly ministerial meeting someone raised the question of the value of newspaper advertisements to a church. A couple of ministers defended them on the basis of their belief that newcomers to the community turned to the Saturday religion page as they began

the process of "church shopping." One of them declared that
any church that did not run an advertisement on the religion
page ran the risk of being left off the lists of these church
shoppers.

At this point one pastor challenged the group by asking,
"Anyone here know of someone who joined a church because
of a church ad in the newspaper?"

After a minute's silence the pastor of Grace United
Methodist Church spoke up and said, "While I'm not
absolutely sure of just why each one joined our congregation, I
believe that at least three dozen of our recent new members
first came to Grace because of our ads in the paper.

"We rarely run an advertisement on the Saturday religion
page, however," he added. "As you may have noticed, our ads
are scattered. One month we place it in the sports section,
another time on the financial pages, another, in the Thursday
food section."

"I've always wondered how you got the newspaper to agree
to that," inquired another minister. "I've been told that the
papers will run church ads only on the Saturday religion page."

"We don't place our ads directly with the newspaper," came
the reply from the pastor at Grace. "We place them through an
advertising agency headed by one of the members of our
congregation. I expect the agency does enough business with
the newspapers here that it has some voice in where the ads
appear," he added drily. "It was their recommendation that we
use more photographs in our ads, run them as a series, finance
the cost through designated second-mile giving, and target a
specific audience with each series of ads. These ads do work for
us."

"We've dropped our advertising from the newspapers,"
commented another pastor. "We decided our problem is not
one of attracting visitors, but rather of welcoming people who
visit our church. For a variety of reasons we get a substantial
number of visitors nearly every Sunday. We take the money we
save on newspaper advertising and run a six-week training
program for our greeters every year. We hire one of these

fellows who trains people to develop their abilities to remember names and faces."

"You mean greeters, or ushers?" asked Don.

"I mean greeters," responded the pastor who was describing this program. "There is a vast difference between an usher and a greeter. The ushers are invited to come to the training program, but all our greeters are required to attend. The church pays the full cost of this training. A week ago a man came who had visited our church about six months ago. One of our greeters went up to him and said, 'Sure good to see you again, Jack! How's Agnes? I remember David and Laura here, but who's this third youngster? She wasn't with you when you were here before.' That's what I mean by there being a difference between an usher and a greeter. Our greeters know how to greet people, and that man was greeted when he came back to Calvary Church."

When he left that meeting of the ministerial association, Pastor Johnson had added two more ideas to the section in his pocket notebook on "winners and losers." He had begun to develop this section of his notebook about two years before he came to St. John's. By Don's definition a "winner" was an idea or procedure or technique that promised creative and productive results, while a "loser" was an approach or procedure that tended to increase the chances of failure, defeat, or frustration.

The first idea that he proposed at St. John's from his "winners" list was in response to the discussion about compensation for lay volunteers and came out of his own experience back at Trinity Church.

In his third year at Trinity, Pastor Johnson and a group of his lay leaders had agreed that everything was running remarkably smoothly. They agreed that one reason was the large corps of active laymen. Out of their discussion came the plan for a special thanksgiving service the first week in January. This special event consisted of four parts. The first was a special worship service in which the congregation gave thanks to God both for the challenges and opportunities in ministry that had been placed before them during the previous twelve months, and for the resources they had been given to respond to these opportunities. The second part consisted of a series of skits, roleplay events, one-act plays, color slides, stunts, vignettes, and a fifteen-minute, 8mm movie. These recaptured most of the highlights of the parish for the past year and were arranged to show the range of programs and ministries at Trinity. The third part was a recognition of the contributions of time, energy, talent, money, and skills that had made possible these programs and ministries. The two-hour evening closed with a presentation showing how the things that had been accomplished during the year just ended provided the foundation for the goals and objectives that had been adopted for the coming year.

When Pastor Johnson broached this idea individually to several of the leaders at St. John's, he received a series of very favorable responses. A few weeks later the subject came up at the monthly church council meeting—the first to be held upstairs in the church parlor incidentally—and was adopted with enthusiasm.

After the council meeting, as he walked down the street to the parsonage, Don was convinced that his first two suggestions at St. John's had received the reception that is necessary for an idea to be a winner. Everyone had agreed that moving the meeting of the church council upstairs to the more comfortable parlor, where everyone could sit in comfortable chairs at tables, rather than in a circle of steel folding chairs in that moldy basement, should have been done long ago. The creative support that had emerged for this thanksgiving service next January suggested that this, too, would be regarded as a winner the morning after the event itself.

While this was not uppermost in his mind as he walked from the church to the parsonage, these two suggestions were, in fact, his second and third winners since arriving at St. John's. The first, and the one that greatly enhanced the chances that any suggestions he made at St. John's would turn out to be winners rather than losers, was the resolution he had made two years earlier while back at Trinity to "pay his rent" promptly every week.

Pastor Johnson's reference to "paying the rent" promptly, comes from James Glasse's suggestion that a congregation wants three things from their minister. They want him to conduct worship and preach, to be their pastor and teacher, and to administer the parish. Glasse contends that (a) paying the rent is not and should not be seen as a full-time job and (b) if the pastor pays his rent promptly every week he has considerable discretion over how he spends the remainder of his time and energy.[2]

Don Johnson had spent most of his time and energy in these first months at St. John's in paying the rent promptly, and he was confident this not only gave him control over how he used his discretionary time, but also helped to produce a favorable climate for innovation. While he had personally met his predecessor only briefly on two different occasions, he had learned that St. John's had not been accustomed to a pastor who paid the rent promptly every week.

As he thought further about the future of his ministry at St. John's, he also became increasingly convinced that the time had come for him to begin to reconsider his leadership role and responsibilities as the new professionally trained leader at St. John's. Don was increasingly open to accepting a more assertive role as an initiating leader. One way of getting more "winners" on the agenda is for the pastor to place them there.

EIGHT

WELL, PASTOR, WHAT DO YOU THINK?

W ell, Pastor, what do you have in mind for us?" inquired Jack Miller, a longtime member of St. John's, of the Reverend Mr. Don Johnson, the recently arrived new minister at St. John's Church.

"I'm afraid it's a little too early for me to respond to that kind of question," replied the new minister. "Tell me, Mr. Miller, what do you see as the most urgent issue St. John's must deal with in the next several months? You've been here for nearly forty years now, compared to only a couple of weeks for me. What do you think are the top priority items on St. John's agenda?"

"You're the minister, I'm just a layman," countered Mr. Miller. "You're the one with all the education and training. We're expecting you to tell us what we should be doing here."

This conversation illustrates one of the most crucial questions to be resolved by the congregation with a new minister. Who will determine the direction this church will go? Who will set the priorities? Who will decide what is at the top of the agenda during that first year?

The vast differences among congregations and the huge variations in the gifts, skills, personalities, and concerns among the clergy mean it is impossible to offer a universal formula that

will fit all situations. It is possible, however, to identify three
very common responses.

The Joint Response

Perhaps the approach preferred by a majority of ministers is
to develop a collaborative arrangement between the newly
arrived pastor and several lay leaders in which they will work
together to determine the agenda and the priorities during that
"honeymoon" year. This was Pastor Johnson's goal when he
had agreed to come to St. John's Church.

While this is an admirable approach, it also may be the most
difficult to implement. In the typical congregation it requires a
minister skilled and comfortable in a collaborative style of
leadership. It also necessitates a cadre of creative and influential
lay leaders who are prepared to invest the time and energy
required to formulate that agenda. It means the congregation is
willing to follow the leadership of that team. This approach rarely
can be followed unless the current agenda is free of the clutter left
over from yesteryear. This clutter may include factionalism or
passivity or a severe financial squeeze or an exodus of members
or large mortgage payments or incompetent staff or just plain
apathy. Perhaps most important of all, it requires a good "match"
between the personality and talents of the new minister and the
interests and priorities of these inherited leaders. This can be a
very productive approach, but it requires a rare combination of
talents and circumstances. At its worst, this approach tempts
people to focus on problems, institutional maintenance, scape-
goating, the past, obstacles to change, and attempts to recreate
yesterday rather than on resources, potentials and the contemporary needs of people—and this also is a risk in a second widely
followed approach to that first year in a new pastorate.

The Reactive Approach

Many ministers prefer to arrive quietly, get acquainted with
the people, discover the distinctive characteristics of their

community, identify some allies, and react to the new situation. That was the approach to his leadership role that Don Johnson had followed at Trinity Church before coming to St. John's.

Frequently this approach is explained or defended by a statement from the newly arrived minister. "It's up to the people here to tell me what they believe should happen. I do not feel I have a right to come in and impose my agenda on them. They've been here a lot longer than I have, it's their church, they will have to live with the consequences after I'm gone, therefore they must determine the priorities and goals."

When asked, "Reverend, what do you think we ought to do?" many of the ministers comfortable with this reactive approach respond, "That's not as important as what you think. What do you want to see happen here?" This is a relatively undemanding leadership role for the new pastor and many ministers appreciate that.

A substantial number of lay people, especially in those smaller congregations averaging eighty-five or fewer at Sunday morning worship, also are very comfortable with this approach. Many of them really prefer a reinforcement of the status quo to an agenda filled with what may appear to be threatening new ideas that a new minister seeks to impose on them.

The Pro-Active Stance

A third approach often is followed by those ministers who are overflowing with creative new ideas, hold and can communicate to others a challenging vision of what could be, are enthusiastic about the potentials of what to them is "my new congregation," possess a strong future orientation, display an aggressive entrepreneurial spirit, lean toward a heavy emphasis on numerical growth and evangelism, are able to inspire others to trust them, possess a high level of self-esteem and self-confidence, are willing to take risks, enjoy an initiating leadership role, are able to inspire others to become allies, and are willing to venture into uncharted waters.[1] The statement,

"But we've never done that here before," is a challenge, not a barrier, to these ministers.

In addition to accepting a different leadership role than is represented by either of the other two approaches, these new ministers also display a sharply different style in the implementation of that more active responsibility. Perhaps the simplest way to illustrate this difference is by the responses to the question, Well, Reverend, what do you think we ought to do next?

These pro-active ministers rarely respond with a non-directive question. Usually they have a highly directive response such as, "It may be time to strengthen the Sunday school," or, "Why don't we try to reach some of the unchurched people here in this community?"

Seven Other Questions

For those recently arrived pastors who prefer a pro-active stance in that first year, these seven questions may be useful responses to that frequently asked, Well, what do you think?

1. How are the finances here?

While this is a means-to-an-end issue, it is placed first for a simple reason. In those congregations that are experiencing a severe financial squeeze, that problem will tend to usurp the agenda. Nothing else will receive the attention it deserves if the treasurer reports we are not able to pay all the bills on time.

If it appears this congregation expects to end the year with a deficit, that first question may be, How do you think we should go about raising the money necessary to eliminate that deficit and when do you think we should do it?

In those congregations with a fiscal year that coincides with the calendar year, the best way to eliminate that impending deficit may be a one-day special financial appeal in late September or early October.

2. What is the procedure here for inviting visitors?

This may be the most important question the newly arrived minister can ask. Most congregations do not have any system for inviting nonmembers to come and share in their fellowship. A heavy emphasis should be given to inviting nonmembers to special programs, events, services, and to new groups. This usually means some form of advertising, which may vary from special mailings to spots on a local radio station to door-to-door visitation to early in the week newspaper advertisements to telephone calls. (See chapter 12 for an elaboration of this point.)

3. Who are the returnees?

It is not at all uncommon for members who have been relatively inactive to make a fresh start with the arrival of a new minister. Since all look like regular attenders on the minister's first Sunday, it may be useful to discover as soon as possible the identity of these returnees. As quickly as possible address them by name and pay them special attention. The best time to reactivate the inactive members is immediately following the arrival of a new minister.

4. Who are the dropouts?

Likewise, when the train stops to pick up a new minister and some of the inactive climb back on, this also may be seen by some of the regular attenders as a good time to drop off into relative inactivity. This is especially common among those who had a very strong allegiance to the former minister and a weak identification with the congregation. The larger the size of the congregation, the easier it is for this to happen without their disappearance being noticed by most of the leaders. Usually the new minister has about six weeks to identify these potential dropouts, establish a personal relationship with them, and rebuild their tie to the church. Staying away from worship can become habit forming after only a few Sundays.

5. Who are our prospective new members?

Sometimes the new minister is handed a list of prospective new members. More often than not, such a list existed only in the head of the predecessor and disappeared when the predecessor left.

A reasonable rule of thumb is that a list of prospective new members should be approximately one-half the length of the list of confirmed members. Thus the 300-member congregation should have a list of at least 140 to 160 constituents and prospective new members. If such a list does not exist, creating it can be a very significant accomplishment during that first year.

6. What are the most distinctive assets and strengths of this congregation?

Many members will be well prepared to greet the new minister with a long list of problems they want the new pastor to solve. The pro-active minister usually will find it more productive to begin by identifying strengths, resources, and assets, and seeking to build on these. This plan was what Don Johnson had selected as one of his "winners" because of his own personal emphasis on an "affirm and build" approach to his leadership responsibilities. The reactive-style pastor may be more comfortable listening to that list of problems.

7. What are the staffing needs here?

A relatively few congregations are staffed to grow, many are staffed to remain on a plateau in size, but most are staffed to decline in size.

Soon after arrival, the new minister may want to raise questions about staffing. Instead of focussing on personalities or jobs, however, it may be more productive to raise questions such as these: Would it be possible for me to have more secretarial help so I could strengthen our system for new member enlistment? Instead of staffing largely or entirely for the care of the present membership, would it be wiser to focus more staff time and energy on prospective new members and community needs? Instead of seeking a part-time youth director, perhaps we should be looking for someone who would specialize in expanding our ministries with families that include teenagers. Instead of a Director of Christian Education, perhaps we need a Program Director who will oversee the entire program, including education.

In general, the larger the size of the congregation, the more likely it is that questions on staffing will and should surface during the first year of a new pastorate. The next chapter describes Don Johnson's efforts to expand the staff at St. John's Church.

Three Cautions

These seven questions are suggested as possible responses when someone asks the new minister, Well, Reverend, what do you think?

There are, however, at least three occasions when asking questions such as these may not be the best approach during that honeymoon year. The most obvious is when the newly arrived pastor discovers the congregation is torn by a severe internal split or respect for the office of pastor has been undermined by actions of the predecessor, or an emergency such as a fire, a flood, or an embezzlement dominates the agenda. In those situations the first priority for the new minister is to heal the division or restore respect for the office of pastor or respond to the emergency.

The second exception allows for those ministers who are extremely uncomfortable with a pro-active leadership role and prefer a nondirective approach to the parish ministry. These ministers really have only four choices. They can enjoy a happy career of serving smaller congregations where a nondirective approach is appropriate and compatible to their leadership role. They can seek to develop an initiating approach to their leadership responsibilities. They can spend a frustration-filled career in the pastoral ministry watching most of the churches they serve drift aimlessly from crisis to crisis. Or they can decide to leave the pastoral ministry for another vocation.

The third is the minister who sees himself or herself as merely passing through and does not want to do anything that will have long-term consequences. If the new minister is unwilling to live with the consequences, or does not expect to stay more than a year or two, it may be unwise to rock the boat by asking leading questions during that first year.

NINE

I NEED HELP!

I need more help!" confided the Reverend Don Johnson to his good friend Betty White. Don was now in his fourth year as the pastor of St. John's Church. During the six years before his arrival, the Sunday morning worship attendance had dropped from an average of 226 to 199. During Don's first year that decline had been reversed and now, four years later, attendance was averaging close to 260, the highest it had ever been.

At Don's insistence, when he had met with the committee to discuss the possibility of coming to St. John's, the leaders had agreed to change from providing twenty-five hours of secretarial service to a full-time, forty-hour-a-week church secretary.

Twice in previous years the leaders at St. John's had employed members as part-time staff members and out of those two experiences had come a policy not to place members on the payroll. The first experience came with a half-time church secretary hired fifteen years earlier. The person the committee had chosen was reasonably competent but had not been employed outside the home for nearly thirty years. She was the wife of a leader who also was a very close friend of the pastor and no problems were ever mentioned. A few years later, however, that minister resigned and was succeeded by the

Reverend Henry Case, Don's immediate predecessor. Within months it became apparent that the new minister and the church secretary not only were incompatible personalities but his expectations of her far exceeded those of the previous minister. Pastor Case insisted her employment be terminated and that he, not a committee, be given the authority to hire a successor. At this time the secretary's husband was (a) an influential member of the church council, (b) still in mourning over the resignation and departure of his close friend, Pastor Case's predecessor, (c) resentful of this trespasser who was intruding on the sacred ground formerly occupied by the husband's close friend, and (d) not at all sympathetic toward the new minister's expectations of his wife as church secretary.

After four months of divisive tension the problem was resolved when (a) the church secretary resigned, (b) the church council granted her three months' terminal leave pay, (c) she and her husband left St. John's to join a new independent congregation on the west edge of town, and (d) Pastor Case was given authority to select a successor and the position was changed from a vague "part-time" role to twenty-five hours a week.

About a year later the Christian education committee, with the full support of Pastor Case, was given the authority to hire someone for twelve to fifteen hours a week to oversee and coordinate the educational program. Nellie Brubaker, a longtime member who had chaired the Christian education committee for several years under Pastor Case's predecessor, was selected for the job. Nellie had taught school for six years before dropping out of the labor force to rear a family. Now, at age fifty-one, her youngest child was seventeen years old and Nellie was interested in a part-time job. She was not under any economic pressure, since her husband, Wesley Brubaker, was a well-to-do insurance agent. Nellie took the newly created position of educational assistant at a modest stipend. The Sunday school superintendent, Herbert Fisher, had agreed to continue for a third year if the church would find a paid staff member to help. He pleaded that as a volunteer he simply did not have the time to do all that needed to be done. Three months later everyone on the educational committee agreed this had been a great decision. Nellie and Herb worked together as a very effective and compatible team.

The following January, however, at the annual meeting when the budget was being presented, three different men generated a big argument over Nellie's position in the budget.

"I have absolutely no question but that Nellie is doing a great job in the Sunday School," declared one man, "but what I want to know is why we are paying our own members to do what always has been done by volunteers?"

"That's a good question," affirmed the next one to get the floor. "I, too, don't question Nellie's great work, but my wife is president of the women's fellowship and she must put in an average of ten to fifteen hours a week on that. Why do we pay one member, but not another?"

"Albert's been the financial secretary here for close to twenty years now; does this mean we'll have to hire someone to take his place when he retires?" questioned someone else.

Before the month was over (a) Nellie had resigned as educational assistant, (b) the church council had adopted a policy that henceforth members would not be put on the payroll, (c) the Christian education committee was furious, and (d) Herbert Fisher had announced that he was resigning as Sunday school superintendent effective May 31.

This experience at St. John's illustrates several lessons. First, it is difficult to find a simple answer to a complex problem.

Second, there really is only one good answer to that question, Why is that person being paid for part-time work here at the church when my wife puts in nearly as much time as a volunteer and doesn't get a nickel for her efforts? The only widely acceptable answer is, We pay her because she is not a member.

Third, unpleasant situations often can be avoided if policy statements are formulated and adopted in advance rather than in reaction to a particular issue.

Fourth, it often is hard to distinguish what appear on the surface to be the real issues from the actual issues hidden beneath the surface, such as personality conflicts and jealousies.

Fifth, when a member is added to the paid program staff of a congregation, this frequently upsets the established pecking order or deference pyramid, and that often is disruptive.

Sixth, nearly every active member is a part of one or more friendship or kinship networks or both, and when a member of one network becomes a member of the paid staff, this can be expected to produce some unpredictable changes in that long established network of relationships. It is also possible that other networks had their own candidates for the position and subsequently define themselves as "losers" in the competition.

Seventh, whenever a well-known member becomes a candidate to fill a vacancy on the church staff, it almost automatically creates some other criteria that will influence the final decision.

Finally, and potentially most troublesome, when a longtime member joins the paid staff, the natural tendency often is to see "my number-one loyalty is to God, my number-two loyalty is to this congregation, which has meant so much to me over the years, and my number-three loyalty is to the staff." It also is not uncommon for the loyalty to that friendship or kinship network to be very high on the list. One pastor with a staff of three part-time program specialists described his situation in these words, "I really don't have what I could call my own staff. What I really find myself doing is trying to work with three individuals, one of whom clearly is the pipeline to and from a group of disgruntled oldtimers, a second is a secret agent of the women's fellowship, and the third really works for her husband who is the church treasurer." Many pastors would prefer that the number one loyalty of each staff member be to the pastor. That not only is good, it is the best relationship if one places a premium on staff harmony, productivity, cooperation, creativity, and healthy interpersonal relationships. (The big exception to these generalizations can be found in those "superchurches" that average well over two thousand at worship on Sunday morning and where anonymity eliminates most of these arguments against hiring members. Many of these congregations have benefitted greatly from rearing *and training* nearly all of their staff from "inside the family.")

That was the background Don Johnson had inherited when

he came to St. John's Church as the new pastor. A few months after he arrived the part-time church secretary announced she and her husband were retiring to Arizona. That left Don with a vacancy as well as permission to seek a full-time church secretary. He also had been instructed that the search must be limited to nonmembers. From the local grapevine Don heard that Lillian West, the wife of the pastor of the Church of the Nazarene on the east side, would prefer working for a church to working in the small factory where she had been employed as secretary for three years.

A Key Staff Position

After interviewing her and four other candidates, Don was convinced Lillian would be an excellent choice. Three years later everyone agreed this had been a perfect decision. Lillian not only served as receptionist, typist, file clerk, and bookkeeper, she also was delighted when the decision was made to install a computer for electronic data and word processing, and she was grateful to St. John's for sending her to the five-day course to learn a new skill.

More important, Lillian was charming on the telephone, served as the alter ego for Pastor Johnson, functioned as the hub of an increasingly complex communications network, understood the nature of the church, coordinated the church calendar, soothed the irritated, recognized that her number one loyalty was to the pastor, had a remarkable memory, foresaw potential crises and conflicts, served as a walking file cabinet, and recognized that it is more important that the work for the day be completed than to leave three minutes early.

Thanks to Lillian, Pastor Johnson had been able to postpone his cry for help, but now the time had come when he concluded he must raise the issue.

The Shrinking Year

One of the reasons that Don Johnson was able to postpone asking for help was the valuable assistance of Lillian West.

Another was he had received a warm welcome from those who were delighted with his positive and enthusiastic approach to ministry. This had increased the corps of hardworking volunteers.

On the other hand St. John's really was staffed for decline, not for growth, ever since Nellie Brubaker's resignation several years earlier. The increase in size, following Don's arrival, simply made the load even larger and heavier. Don had been able to get by, partly due to the fact that he is an unusually productive worker and partly because he was new.

Many pastors will agree the first year of a new pastorate seems to be about 700 days long and the second year is closer to 500 days. By the time the third year rolls around, one's discretionary time has largely disappeared and it seems more like 300 days from Christmas to Christmas. By the ninth year it feels like Easter comes once every 150 days.

Thus Don's plea for more help was partly the normal response of a minister in a large, "awkward-sized," and understaffed congregation.[1] In part it was the plea of a minister who no longer had any discretionary time for the inevitable "extras" that come up unexpectedly.

"What kind of help do you want?" responded Betty White to Don's plea for a new staff position. "Do you want an associate minister or should we look for an intern from the seminary who could come on a full-time basis for a year? That might be the best way to make the transition to a second full-time program person and it wouldn't cost as much as a full-time ordained minister. Or maybe we should look for a retired minister who could take most of the calling off your shoulder."

"I'm not sure what I want," replied Don. "I'm sure of only four aspects of the situation. First, I know I need more help. Second, I don't want to surrender all the calling to a part-time retired minister. I enjoy that and I believe I do a good job in that part of my ministry.

"Third, I know I don't want a seminary intern. I've talked to too many pastors who have had interns. They all agree that about the time an intern really begins to be productive, it is time to return to the seminary. I believe we need more continuity than an intern can offer. Besides the lack of continuity, many of my friends argue they spend as much time supervising and meeting with the intern as they get back in productivity from the intern's work.

"Fourth, I know we need someone to help with program, not with the administration. Administration is one of those things that fills up all the time that is available. Lillian is in fact my administrative assistant, even though her title is church secretary, and I don't want to disturb her role by bringing in a part-time administrator."

"Do you want a specialist or a generalist?" asked Betty. "Perhaps that would be the best beginning point for exploring the idea of more staff."

Generalist or Specialist?

For many congregations averaging between 160 and 300 at worship on Sunday morning, the top three priorities in building a staff team are:

1. A full-time ordained minister.
2. A church secretary who resembles Lillian West.
3. The generalist who will be able to fulfill several responsibilities.

At St. John's Church, for example, a good case could be made for adding a full-time, or perhaps three-quarter time, professional staff person who would (a) serve as director of program, (b) recognize and help to meet the need for an expansion of program, (c) accept a leadership role in initiating new ministries, (d) direct a leadership development process to provide lay volunteer staff for these new ministries, (e) not be perceived as a threat or rival by the senior minister, (f) not feel the need to preach on a dozen or more Sundays every year, (g) provide a sense of continuity when the day comes that Don Johnson leaves St. John's, and (h) stay in that staff position for at least seven to twelve years.

This person could be either ordained or lay. Given the pressures on many of the clergy "to have your own church" and the limited career possibilities for the ordained associate minister, the growing trend is for this position to be filled by a diaconal minister or a layperson.

In the very large congregations this probably must be a full-time position, but in those churches averaging fewer than 300 at worship, it often can be filled effectively by a part-time person.

An alternative at St. John's would be to consider a two- or three- or four-stage program for expanding the staff. Instead of adding one full-time staff person to create a staff team of three, with Don and Lillian, it might be wise to add, on a one-at-a-time basis, two or three or four part-time specialists, each of whom would be on a more limited part-time basis. The dollar cost probably would be less than adding an inexperienced, full-time ordained minister to the staff, the productivity might be greater, and in all probability Don Johnson, like most pastors, would find it easier to oversee and relate to three part-time specialists than to one full-time generalist.

What would these part-time specialists do? That question would have to be answered by the leaders at St. John's Church, but a dozen possibilities can be identified from what we know about this congregation.

1. The part-time specialist who would concentrate on improving the process for the assimilation of new members. In the majority of Protestant congregations one-fourth to one-half of all new members drop into inactivity within two years after uniting with their church. At St. John's this might be a ten- to twelve-hours-per-week position.

2. A part-time specialist in leadership development who would expand, oversee, and nurture the network of volunteers at St. John's, placing special emphasis on helping people enhance their own personal and spiritual growth through volunteer service, rather than simply identifying bodies to fill vacant positions.

3. A part-time program director for what was a middle-sized congregation and is now in the process of becoming a large church.

4. A staff person to organize and oversee a comprehensive new-member enlistment program.

5. A mature adult to enlist a cadre of volunteers for a ministry with families that have teenagers.

6. A specialist in ministries with children and their families.

7. A part-time educational assistant to enlist and direct a corps of volunteers in a comprehensive Christian education program. This was the position Nellie Brubaker had filled many years earlier.

8. Someone with the vision to develop specialized ministries with those who are overlooked by most churches, such as families with a handicapped child, single parents, the recently widowed, young adults who have never married but who do not want to be categorized by their marital status, persons who do not speak English, the hearing impaired, the recently divorced, or the new stepparents.

9. One with a vision of the church that includes the whole planet, who can inspire others to see that vision, and can translate that vision into operational mission and ministry.

10. That gifted person who believes in the need for a woman's organization and who can enlist women of all ages in the mission and outreach of the women's organization.

11. The part-time parish visitor who calls and calls and calls.

12. The part-time minister of music who, instead of organizing and directing one or two vocal choirs, organizes a team of volunteers who share in organizing and directing a music program that includes vocal choirs, specialized instrumental groups, such as a handbell choir or a flute group or a brass quartet, an annual dramatic presentation and perhaps even an orchestra.

Why Not Lay Volunteers?

When Betty and Don presented to the church council at St. John's the idea of expanding the program staff, the first response came from a sixty-one-year-old, longtime leader: "Why do we have to hire someone? Why can't we use lay volunteers? Our congregation today is larger than it's ever been in the thirty years I've been a member here. It seems to me a church loses a bit of vitality when it hires people to do what volunteers can and should do."

That is a common response to a proposal to expand staff. In reflecting on it, these observations from experience should be added to the discussion.

First, and most significant, with rare exceptions the churches that have the best network of lay volunteers in a variety of program areas are those that are fully staffed. The evidence suggests that a well-paid program staff and a large number of lay volunteers are not alternative courses of action, they are complementary. The assistance, the continuity, the availability, and the skills of the paid staff are foundation stones for building a comprehensive network of lay volunteers.

A second factor is the time required. Each of the twelve positions described earlier requires somewhere between 600 and 2600 hours a year. Few volunteers have both the gifts and that much time. Furthermore, these are all program positions. Most of our churches are organized to direct lay volunteers in administrative roles such as finance or other means-to-an-end assignments. In addition, the rapid growth in the number of families in which both the husband and wife are employed outside the home has curtailed a major source of volunteers. Can churches turn the calendar back to the 1950s and the 1930s?

In 1986 the financial compensation for these positions varied from $100 a month to $35,000 a year, and most of the part-time program specialists were in the $2,500- to $9,000-a-year range. Scores of churches have created three to six part-time positions, each of which pays $2,000 to $4,500 a year. Most of these positions are filled by women who otherwise would not be employed outside the home. From the employee's perspective one advantage is the opportunity to begin an Individual Retirement Account (IRA).

It is not uncommmon to find a congregation with four or five part-time lay specialists with a combined compensation total of less than $20,000. That is significantly less than the total compensation for the typical full-time ordained associate minister. In other words, one reason this is an increasingly attractive alternative is it often costs less than bringing a full-time seminary graduate on to the staff.

A fourth factor behind the increase in the number of part-time lay specialists on church staffs is a larger societal trend. Increasingly our society is turning to specialists in agriculture, medicine, education, automobile repairs, the law, real estate, and dozens of other areas of life. It should not be surprising to find the churches turning to specialists rather than to generalists, especially if it is cheaper.

Another very influential factor has been the emergence of the church growth movement and the recognition by many congregations of the value of an extensive program to reinforce the evangelistic outreach of that parish. A large proportion of these congregations cannot afford a large number of full-time program staff persons, so they seek part-time specialists. This trend can be seen most clearly in those congregations and denominations that have decided to make a major effort to reach, attract, receive, and assimilate members of the generation born in the 1950–1965 era. In disproportionately large numbers this generation of adults can be found in large congregations that have extensive program and a large staff, many of whom are part-time program specialists.

Finally, St. John's had made a conscious and deliberate decision to reach more people. This meant an increase in the workload in planning and developing new ministries, in identifying and enlisting a larger cadre of volunteers, in the pastoral care of this larger number of members, and in the administrative burden. More people means more work—and that should mean a larger staff.

Who Are the Candidates?

Where can St. John's turn to find people who will fill some of these specialized program positions?

The vast majority of part-time specialists who are making a superb contribution usually fit one of three categories. An increasing number are older adults, including a great many men who have retired from a secular job, do not want or need a full-time job and are delighted to find this opportunity open to them. Today one out of every four males in the 55–59 age bracket identifies himself as "retired."

The largest group are mothers who have passed their 40th (often their 60th) birthday, who are not tied to the home by young children, who have gifts of creativity and organizational abilities, who neither need nor want a full-time job, who like people, who have good interpersonal skills, who find fulfillment in this role, who have not been professionally trained for a religious vocation, and who are committed both to the Christian faith and to the worshipping congregation. A very large proportion of these women are not currently married.

The third group comes from that growing number of Americans who choose to have two jobs at the same time. This list includes the banker who is a remarkably creative minister of music, the junior high social studies teacher who has built an excellent ministry with families that have teenagers, the nurse who directs the specialized ministry with families that have a Down Syndrome child, the physicist who oversees the adult Christian education program in a very large church, the cabinetmaker who has organized a team of forty lay volunteers to do visitation evangelism, and the attorney who leaves the office at two o'clock nearly every Wednesday afternoon to oversee the Youth Club program in that Presbyterian church.

While it took nearly a year for the leaders at St. John's to adopt a program for the expansion of the staff, by the end of Don Johnson's sixth year the staff included Don, Lillian, a fifty-eight-year-old widow who was the half-time program director, a retired fifty-seven-year-old widower who was paid for fifteen hours a week to direct a new member enlistment program (he actually worked an average of fifty hours a week), and a thirty-seven-year-old nurse with a full-time job at the local hospital who was paid for twelve hours a week to oversee and expand the efforts in the assimilation of new members.

This decision had several unexpected results. First, while Pastor Johnson's total work load was not reduced as he and some of the leaders at St. John's had hoped, for the first year or so, the expansion of the staff did allow Don to spend more time doing what he most enjoyed doing and what he thought he did best. Second, the program grew rather rapidly, thanks to the addition of a part-time program director. Third, to the dismay of many, while the congregation experienced a substantial increase in the number of new members received each year, the number dropping into inactivity increased even more rapidly. This was the predictable result of a part-time staff person, who really worked full-time, building an effective system for the enlistment of new members, while another staff member invested only twelve hours a week expanding the efforts to assimilate new members.

Fourth, as the years flew by, Pastor Johnson found himself spending more time in the office and less time out calling. He had come to St. John's to serve as the pastor of a numerically declining congregation. Now he was the senior minister of a substantially larger parish with a hardworking and dedicated staff who looked to him for leadership, direction, advice, and ideas. The burdens of administration continued to grow and less and less time was available each year for what Don preferred to do.

Fifth, both Pastor Johnson and the leaders had to deal with the fact that life at St. John's was growing more complicated. Disputes over priorities in the use of rooms, over what had the top priority on an individual's time and energy, and over who should attend which committee meeting proliferated. During his first couple of years at St. John's, Pastor Johnson rarely thought or planned more than ten or fifteen months in advance. During his eighth year all the staff agreed the standard twelve-month calendar on the wall near Lillian's desk must be replaced with a twenty-four- or thirty-month calendar.

Finally, while no one had even thought about this, the acceleration in the pace of congregational life, the expansion of the program, the influx of strangers who acted as though they had all the rights and privileges of longtime members, the growth in the complexity of and the decrease in the time Don had to spend with longtime members coincided with the gradual disappearance of several members who had formerly been influential leaders. Some identified a cause-and-effect relationship while others did not even notice the disappearance of these former leaders.

Earlier a friend of Don's on the staff of the regional judicatory had warned, "Don, you'll learn that one of the price tags of growth is a higher turnover in your membership and some of your longtime leaders will be among those who leave."

Don had been shocked when he first received this advice, but now he knew it reflected reality. The positive side of that pattern was that the worship attendance climbed substantially even though the membership total changed only slightly. The negative side was that Don could not be comfortable with former leaders dropping out.

TEN

WHAT HAPPENS
TO THE
EX-LEADERS?

Joe Ferguson taught the high school Sunday school class here for five or six years. Toward the end of that period, he was one of the key members of our finance committee and he served on that committee for six years. He next served two terms on our church council and was president of the council for the last two years. He also helped with a lot of other things around here. When Myra and I joined St. John's nineteen years ago, I soon discovered Joe was one of the most reliable, committed, and respected leaders of this congregation," recalled Clint Townsend, a member of St. John's Church. He and his wife, Myra, were talking with Gene and Alice Copeland one Saturday after dinner in the Copeland's home. These two couples were longtime members of St. John's, close friends, and usually got together once or twice a month for a meal and fellowship.

"About five years ago he finished up his second term as president of the church council," continued Clint. "During the past several months Joe gradually has dropped out of everything here and now he only comes to church about once a month. I've stopped to see him on three different occasions. Each time he was very friendly and claimed everything was fine. The Sunday following each visit he would be back in church, but then I wouldn't see him for maybe a month. What happens with people like that?"

"I guess I've seen that same pattern with several other members here at St. John's," recalled Gene Copeland. "We've had folks who were very heavily involved for years and years. Then one day, usually after they've completed a term in office or some other obligation, they simply drop out. I'm not talking about those who move away. I'm referring to those who continue to live at the same address, but, for all practical purposes, drop out of church."

"What you're talking about has now been identified as burnout," diagnosed Alice Copeland, a registered nurse. "We overload people, we ask them to accept responsibilities with which they are not comfortable, and we ask them to give until they're exhausted. Gradually they begin to see leadership in the church as a burden, rather than as a channel for expressing their commitment to Jesus Christ. Too often they feel starved for spiritual nourishment. Worship no longer is a spiritually renewing experience. Frequently these folks come to church on Sunday morning with a list of people they have to see or things they have to do, and they're not able to concentrate on the experience of worship. The church is notorious for asking people to give of themselves until they're simply burned out."

"That's true. There's no question the church does exploit a lot of willing people," agreed Myra Townsend. "But I don't think that applies to Joe Ferguson and I've tried to explain this to you before, Clint, but you wouldn't listen. You're always too judgmental of other people.

"Joe happens to be a good friend of mine and his store is right next to my shop downtown," continued Myra, who owns and operates a small gift shop. "I don't think he represents a case of burnout. A little over five years ago Joe was elected president of the Chamber of Commerce. He confided to me that he wasn't sure he should take that responsibility because at that same time he was getting ready to open a new store out in the new shopping center on the east side of town. He also added that the only reason he even considered it was that he was within a couple of months of completing his last year as president of your church council.

"I don't disagree with Alice about the dangers of burnout," continued Myra, "but I think Joe Ferguson represents another phenomenon.

"One way to explain it," she continued, "is to look at how preachers outline a sermon or public speakers outline a speech. I was taught that every speech should have a beginning, a middle, and a conclusion. That's all people can remember. If you go beyond three points, you ask more of people than they can remember. Likewise, many people cannot participate in more than three circles of life at the same time. Joe is a wonderful family man. He and his wife have five children, two of whom are still at home. One circle of his life consists of his family. Another is his business next door to my downtown shop. The third was the church. When he expanded the second circle by opening a new store and when he moved from chairing a committee in the chamber to becoming president of that organization, he created a fourth big circle. Something had to give. It couldn't be his family or his business, so that third circle, the church, had to shrink in size."

"That's a new one to me," admitted Gene Copeland, "but I guess you have a good point there. A lot of people do get involved in something new and when they do, something else gets squeezed out of their lives. I recall when our oldest daughter was studying for the bar exams several years ago, she dropped everything else for about six weeks including her boyfriend, church, us, and anything that wouldn't help her pass those exams."

"That's the point," agreed Myra. "There's nothing magic about three circles. That's really not the issue. Perhaps a better way to put it is the concept of a fixed sum of time and energy. Each one of us is limited to twenty-four hours in one day. If we devote more time to a new interest, something else has to receive less time."

"I've always believed in the old adage that the best way to get someone active in any organization, or to reactivate those who have dropped out is to ask them to take a job," offered Alice

Copeland. "If they have a job to do, they get active. Why doesn't the nominating committee ask Joe to take a position on some committee where he'll know he will be useful, but it won't be as much work or demand as much time as the church council requires?"

"I thought of that," agreed Clint, "and last fall, when I was finishing my term on the nominating committee, I suggested Joe's name for two different vacancies we were trying to fill. What stunned me was that two members of the nominating committee claimed they didn't know Joe Ferguson. I was flabbergasted! How anyone can be a member of St. John's and not know good old Joe really amazed me. Both of those folks are relatively new, of course; they both joined within the past couple of years, but I couldn't believe they were on the nominating committee and didn't know Joe Ferguson. I guess 'out of sight, out of mind' does describe our world today."

* * *

This conversation illustrates two themes. One is the disappearance from high visibility and active involvement of persons who formerly were among the hardest working members of a congregation. A second theme is the speculation about why this happens. The missing theme is what can be done about it.

Why Does It Happen?

The easy dropout to explain is the homemaker who is a hardworking volunteer, sees her youngest child enter senior high, finds full-time employment outside the home, and reduces her involvement in church activities from ten or fifteen to one or two hours a week. The hard one to explain is the busy man who managed his time very carefully, spent fifty or sixty hours a week on the job, including the journey to and from work, devoted a fair amount of time to his family, gave five to fifteen hours a week to the church, retired, and today is rarely seen around the parish.

For some this drop in their degree of involvement in the church does represent what is now described as burnout. For others it represents a change in the priorities on their time. Something else requires more time and so less is available for the church. Apparently that is what happened to Joe Ferguson.

For many this decrease in involvement can be explained in relational terms. The influential leader who chaired the committee seeking a new minister stakes that earned reputation on the credentials of the recommended candidate who is called. Subsequently that leader becomes disillusioned with the new minister (sometimes because the new minister refuses to become dependent on that leader's advice) and drops out. Sometimes the person who was an articulate advocate of new programs, such as church growth, did not realize that change rarely comes without unanticipated consequences. The disillusioning discovery that "there is no gain without pain" may be the decisive factor in causing the former advocate of change to drop out.

A young couple move into the community, join the church, become heavily involved in the life of that congregation, meet and make new friends, greet the arrival of their first child, and suddenly discover they are very short of the discretionary time that had enabled them to be such heavily involved volunteers. They no longer feel the need for new friends, and soon become less visible in the church. Sometimes divorce is the reason one spouse disappears from the church scene.

Without intending to develop this progression, some congregations ask members to serve as volunteer workers and subsequently "promote" several to serve as policy makers on committees and boards. A few of these eventually are asked to move into important leadership roles. The result appears to resemble a pyramid with the most influential lay leader role at the peak of that pyramid. Most of the responses to faithful volunteers can be assigned to one of four categories: (1) expressions of gratitude, (2) requests to accept additional obligations, (3) "promotion" to greater responsibilities, and (4) no discernible response. The most obvious next step for those leaders who have fulfilled their term at the top of that pyramid is to accept the expressions of gratitude and drop into inactivity. The system does not include the alternative of demotion to a less prestigious role for that volunteer.

While some people dread the thought of retirement, others look forward to it. For some, retirement promises a welcome change of pace and a shedding of old responsibilities. Sometimes that includes terminating leadership responsibilities in the church in favor of travel, more time with the grandchildren, a new spouse, a new volunteer role in some other organization, or in order to be free of all obligations.

Perhaps the most widely discussed factor that produces ex-leaders is the move to a new stage in the life cycle. This may be the arrival of a new baby, the confirmation of the youngest child, divorce, taking a second job, the departure of the youngest child from home, widowhood, the onset of health problems, retirement, or the move to a new community. Each new stage provides a justification for the termination of leadership responsibilities.

What Is Our Response?

While it is impossible to identify all the factors behind the dropping out of ex-leaders, it is possible to suggest several positive responses.

First, make sure every ex-leader receives an expression of gratitude that goes beyond a few spoken words of appreciation. This may range from a note from the pastor to a pin to a gift to a certificate of thanks to a photograph to a luncheon or dinner to a party to formal recognition at some major event at the church.

Second, consider enriching the spiritual journey of ex-leaders. This could involve the organization of a new Bible study group, or asking an ex-leader to specialize in some phase of the biblical narrative and become the resident expert who teaches that subject, or the creation of a new prayer group, or serving as a liturgist on Sunday morning or occasionally preaching in that small congregation twelve miles west of here that does not have a minister, or serving as a counsellor at youth camp, or enhancing the emphasis on the identification and nurture of an individual's spiritual gifts, or organizing a new group that focusses on adult faith development.

Third, ask someone, and the pastor may not always be the best one to do this, to conduct an exit interview with each person who is vacating a leadership role. The exit interview should include questions such as, What did you learn during your term of office that can benefit all of us? If you were doing it over again, how would you do it differently? How could we improve the nurture of our leaders here? What was your point of greatest frustration? What was your greatest satisfaction while serving in this leadership role? The feedback from these exit interviews to current leaders should be anonymous.

Fourth, keep those ex-leaders informed! A common complaint is, When you're not on the board, you really don't know what's going on around here. Improve the quality of the communication process for the ex-leaders.

Fifth, seek the counsel of ex-leaders. "Joe, what do you think about this proposal?" Ex-leaders often have valuable advice that not only should be heard, but often improves the decision-making process. It is not unusual to find three or four former leaders who continue as very active members. For each the secret is, I'm the number-one confidential adviser to our new minister, but no one else knows it.

Finally, when the occasion presents itself, and sometimes the occasion must be created, ask the ex-leader who has moved to the sidelines to chair or co-chair a short-term special event that has high visibility, is important, has a terminal date, and will be a happy experience for all. "Joe, would you chair the committee to plan the celebration of our one hundredth anniversary?" "Bertha, the second of this September marks the tenth anniversary of Helen's first day as our church secretary. Would you chair a committee that will oversee the celebration of that occasion?" "Chris, would you be willing to take the responsibility for planning something that will express our appreciation to the choir?" "Ian, those front steps are about to fall apart. Would you organize a committee to replace them?"

"Mickey, our congregation has agreed to host this big denominational meeting next October. Would you be willing to co-chair the special arrangements committee?"

Among the key characteristics of these special responsibilities are (1) they are short-term, (2) they have a clearly defined terminal date, (3) they have high visibility, (4) they include fun events or happy experiences, and (5) they require and encourage creativity.

What do you do to nurture your ex-leaders? Please do not neglect them.

ELEVEN

WHO'S IN CHARGE HERE?

I 'm sorry I can't take you into our new church parlor," said Jack Taylor to his old college classmate Don Johnson, "but there's only one key. The women raised the money for this room and bought the furnishings—and the president of our church women's organization has the only key. If you stand over here, however, you can see part of the inside of the room through this window. They did a tremendous job of decorating and furnishing it and it's the most attractive room in the whole building."

Don had stopped by to pick up Jack and another pastor for the four-hour drive to the annual denominational pastor's school. They had agreed to meet at Jack's and they were taking a quick tour of the new building before going on their way.

As they continued through the new structure, Tom Wilson, an associate minister in the 3,300-member Calvary Church on the other side of the city, commented with envy, "This is a beauty of a fellowship hall! You have fewer than a fourth as many members as we have at Calvary, but we don't have anything that can begin to compare with this." As he looked around at the beautifully decorated, carpeted, and softly lighted, seventy-foot-long room, he added, "This is just what we needed last Saturday. The daughter of one of our most active members was married in the church, but the wedding reception was held downtown in a hotel, because our fellowship hall is too small and too noisy to accommodate a large crowd. You get two or three hundred people in there all talking at once, and you can't hear yourself think, the way the noise bounces off the walls and ceilings."

"We had a big wedding reception in here shortly after we moved into the building," replied Jack Taylor, "and that ended that. It took our custodian most of a day to get the cake out of the rug. The trustees have decided that no refreshments can be served in here, so now we use that double classroom across the hall that has a folding door in the middle for any kind of group that has refreshments."

"Who did you say made that policy?" asked Tom Wilson, "the custodian or the trustees?"

"The trustees, of course," began Jack Taylor. "Oh, I see your point now. Well, to be more precise, I guess you can say the policy was initiated by the custodian and approved by the trustees."

This conversation illustrates one of the most important issues in the parish today. It is an issue that often divides laymen, frequently pits the people against the pastor, and usually causes many needless misunderstandings. It can be compressed into five words: *Who is in charge here?*

In most congregations many people give widely varying answers to that question and, even more significantly, often articulate one set of answers but are guided in their actions by another.

One method of surfacing this issue is to list on a sheet of paper eight or ten or a dozen factors that appear to be the most influential in the decision-making process in a particular congregation. In one congregation, this sheet was circulated among the twenty members of the governing body of the congregation.

Who's in Charge Here?

You have 100 points to divide up among these factors, which influence the decision-making process here at Church Street

Church. Allocate the appropriate number of points to each influence or factor. Make sure they total exactly 100.

Influence	*Percentage Points*
Tradition	
The pastor	.
The church school	
The Holy Spirit	
Goals	
A dozen old-timers	
Location	
The building	
Financial limitations	
The church council	
Size	
Other (write in)	_____
TOTAL	100%

Each member of the governing body was given a copy of this sheet and asked to identify and weigh the importance of each factor by indicating the relative importance of each item. One layman, for example, wrote 30 percent after tradition, gave 35 percent to the influence of the pastor, 2 percent each to the Holy Spirit, goals, location, size, and a dozen old-timers, 5 percent to the building, 10 percent to the church council, and the remaining 10 percentage points he assigned to financial limitations.

After each member had completed the assignment, the sheets were collected. Both the range and the average were calculated for each item, including the write-ins under "other."

In one 1,700-member downtown congregation the results of this tabulation, using a similar form but with a slightly different set of items, looked like this when reproduced for discussion by the governing body:

Who's in Charge at First Church?

Average*	Influence	Range of Values**
8	Tradition	0 to 20
7	Building	0 to 40
14	Location	5 to 70
6	Stained-glass windows	0 to 20
2	The radio broadcast	0 to 40
1	Goals	0 to 10
9	Music and the choir	5 to 25
10	Financial limitations	0 to 70
8	Perceived needs of people	0 to 30
3	The Holy Spirit	0 to 60
7	Ten key lay leaders	0 to 30
20	The pastor	5 to 80
5	Others (write-ins)	1 to 30

*The "average" is the arithmetic mean, arrived at by adding the total points assigned to each item and dividing by the number of papers turned in.
**The "range" simply reports the lowest and the highest number assigned to each item.

The use of this procedure in a 300-member congregation in a rural community of 4,600 residents resulted in this summary:

Who's in Charge at Grace Church?

Average	Influence	Range
4	The nature of this community	0 to 40
8	The Holy Spirit	0 to 30
12	The building	5 to 50
4	The National Football League*	0 to 20
6	The choir	2 to 17
13	Tradition	10 to 60
5	A widespread conservatism	0 to 70
26	The minister	15 to 80
7	The Sunday school	0 to 20
3	The women's organization	0 to 30
9	The lakes*	0 to 40
3	Apathy	0 to 16

*In this congregation, as in many others, it was openly recognized that the schedule of the televised games of the National Football League in the fall had influenced the church schedule for all day Sunday as well as for Monday evening, while the attractiveness of the nearby lakes was a major force all summer long.

This same procedure was used by a 90-member, open-country church; the responses from twenty-two leaders, including several teenagers, are reproduced in this summary:

Who's in Charge at Oak Grove Church?

Average	Influence	Range
12	The preacher	0 to 70
38	The cemetery	5 to 60
8	The church council	5 to 15
19	Four laymen	0 to 60
18	Yesterday	0 to 80
5	The Holy Spirit	0 to 15

It is important to tailor the categories to fit each situation. This can be illustrated by comparing the categories used at Oak Grove and at St. Luke's, a 1,785-member, suburban congregation in a southern metropolitan area.

Who's in Charge at St. Luke's Church?

Average	Influence	Range
3	Location	0 to 15
10	Building facilities	5 to 25
3	The Bible	0 to 10
14	The heavy emphasis on program	0 to 60
5	Financial limitations	0 to 80
8	The music program	5 to 35
6	The church school schedule	0 to 62

Average	Influence	Range
4	The Holy Spirit	0 to 45
17	The senior minister	5 to 80
2	Traditions	0 to 10
4	The business manager	0 to 30
11	Response to human need	0 to 50
5	Goals	0 to 38
8	A lack of trust	0 to 65

In using this procedure it is helpful to prepare a list and ask everyone to work from the same list. A simple, open-ended questionnaire will provide some interesting responses, but these responses are nearly impossible to tabulate in a meaningful manner that can be used for subsequent discussion. The use of a form "depersonalizes" the responses and reduces the degree of defensiveness in any subsequent discussion.

There are several ways of building the list that will be circulated. One is to interview persons individually and use an open-ended question like, Who's in charge around here, how are decisions made, and who or what influences what this church does and how it does it? Another method is to ask a group of people what has been happening and attempt to perceive why certain decisions came out the way they did. A fourth is to ask four or five people to build lists separately and then produce a composite. A fifth is to combine the first four approaches.

This procedure has several values for the pastor and the people who want to increase the degree of intentionality in the decision-making process in their parish, to help one another understand the differences among people, or to accelerate the pace of planned change.

One of the most obvious values of this procedure is that it quickly reveals any discrepancies that may exist among the people or between a leadership group and the pastor in how they perceive the decision-making process to operate. If the discrepancy is large, this procedure opens up opportunities for creative discussion.

Perhaps more important is the discrepancy between the ideal and reality. While a few people will respond with idealized interpretations of the influences on the decision-making process, most people tend to be very frank and realistic in describing what they perceive to be the active forces at work. For example, only rarely do either "the Holy Spirit" or "goals" secure more than 5 or 10 points each in the composite score of a group of fifteen or twenty parish leaders. This procedure almost automatically produces an identification of the discrepancy between "the way it is here" and "the way it ought to be here." The resulting discontent is the essential first step in planned change.[1] It may be useful to ask people to work through this process twice. The first time they can be asked to respond to the question, Who really is in charge here? The second time the question can be changed to, Who should be in charge here? or, What would be the ideal distribution of influence in how decisions are made here?

A third value in the use of this simple procedure is that it enables people, and especially a new pastor, to gain very quickly an idea of how others see the local situation and of the reality with which he or she is confronted.

This procedure is also a very helpful tool for the layperson or minister who is consciously interested in the question of leadership style. By including four or five items such as "the pastor," "a small group of very influential laymen," "the church council," "properly elected and designated leaders," "three families," or "the pastor and two or three of his very close allies," it is possible to discover what people *believe* to be the current style or pattern of leadership in the parish. What people believe to be reality, rather than reality itself, often is the best beginning point for planning changes.

If the parish has both a program-planning committee or council and a separate administrative board, it may be helpful to ask each group to participate separately in this exercise, and then to compare the composite scores of the two groups. Occasionally this is very revealing.

Finally, this procedure is one of the doors that can lead to a creative discussion of purpose, of the reason for the existence of *this* parish, and of the distinction between ends (goals) and the means to an end.

TWELVE

WHERE ARE
THE VISITORS?

W ell, Pastor, what do you think we should be doing?" asked Sylvia Potter, who had been chairing the evangelism committee at St. John's for the past four years. "Do you have anything you want us to discuss this evening?" Pastor Don Johnson had arrived only a few weeks earlier and this was his first meeting with the evangelism committee.

"I guess my first question is, How often do you meet? and the second is, What do you see as your basic responsibilities?" replied Pastor Johnson.

"We haven't been meeting as often as I suppose we should," explained Sylvia somewhat defensively, "but we really haven't had much to do. Our basic responsibility is to call on all the people who visit us on Sunday. As you know, every Sunday we ask the visitors to sign a pew card and place it in the offering plate. One of the ushers gives those cards to me. If anyone checks the box on the card indicating interest in becoming a member, I pass the card on to one of the members of my committee to call on that person or family. Sometimes I go ahead and make the call myself. Our problem is we haven't had much business. On over half of the Sundays during the year we don't have any visitors, and less than half of those who do visit check the box indicating they want a visit."

"Well, I've only been here for seven Sundays now, but my impression has been that we've had visitors every week," commented Don. "Is that unusual?"

"Yes, you are right," replied Sylvia, "but most of those were out-of-town relatives visiting some of our members, and they're really not prospective new members. I thought you might ask about that, and I have the cards here for every local visitor since you came. All told, there are nine. One is a new family in town and I called on them the day after they first came. They've been here every Sunday now and I know you've called on them twice. Three are cards for visitors who have been here before and five are first-time visitors, but only one of those five checked they wanted a call. That means we've had five calls to make in seven weeks. While that's about double the rate it was before you came, it is really not very many. That's why I said we don't have a lot of business."

"Maybe this is a good beginning point for our discussion tonight," urged Don. "It seems to me there are two aspects of this business about Sunday morning visitors that we should talk about. The first is a minor detail and I can take care of it myself if I have your permission. Can we change the pew card? I would like to change only one item. The card now has a box to be marked after the sentence reading, 'Are you interested in becoming a member of St. John's Church?' I would like to have a new batch of cards printed in which that would be changed to read, 'Would you like to talk with someone about the possibility of joining St. John's?' I think that would open the door for more visits."

"I don't see any reason why we couldn't do that," agreed Sylvia.

"How many of the old cards do we have on hand?" inquired Amos Verhoef, a sixty-five-year-old member of the committee who rarely spoke. "Perhaps we should use up all the cards we have on hand first and make that change in the next order."

"I think we're about out of these cards," lied Sylvia who knew she had close to a thousand at home in a cupboard. "Does anyone else have any other changes to suggest before we order a new printing? If you do, let me know before the first of next month. If it's all right with the committee, I'll get together with our pastor and we'll design a card for the new printing. What's the second item you wanted to talk to us about, Pastor?"

"The second is a far bigger and more important one," continued Don, who was barely able to suppress his delight with how Sylvia had been able to keep the discussion on the pew card from continuing for another hour. "This is the issue of how we can increase the number of first-time visitors who might be prospective new members. I think our goal should be at least a hundred first-time visitors from among local residents during the next year."

"That sounds good to me," affirmed Sylvia. "Do you have some ideas on how we can pull that off?"

"Well, I think we might begin by seeing how we can make our property more inviting."

"That's the trustee's job, not ours," protested Ian MacGregor. "I don't think we should trespass on the responsibilities of the trustees. We've got enough to do without taking on the responsibilities of some other committee!"

Despite this jurisdictional question, Don had a good point. Any congregation increasing the number of first-time visitors might begin by looking at the message the property conveys to those prospective visitors.

What Does the Building Say?

Where is the building located? Is it on a heavily travelled road or street? Does the property invite strangers to stop? Is the entrance to the parking lot easy to find? Is offstreet parking available? If yes, is it easily seen from the street? Does the building have a clearly identified and inviting main entrance? Or do the members mostly come in through an uninviting rear entrance from the parking area? Is there a sign or bulletin board near the street that identifies the name of the church, the denominational affiliation, and the Sunday morning schedule? Does it include the pastor's name and telephone number? Can this sign be read easily by a motorist in a passing automobile? If the meeting place does not have high visibility, are there signs on major streets and intersections directing strangers to your church? (If the building sets back from the street and is partially obscured by nearby structures, is there a sign or bulletin board out near the street?) If the building "does not look like a church," is a cross or some other symbol prominently displayed to help identify this as your meeting place?

If a stranger does come, does the building itself direct the person to the proper entrance? Or do you have exterior signs to guide the stranger? What does the newcomer find after entering the building? Is the design of the building such that a stranger can easily find the church offices or the sanctuary or the appropriate classroom? Or do you have interior directional signs?

"Let's assume we can persuade the trustees to spend money on signs and on making our building more attractive. What else do we need to bring more visitors to St. John's?" asked Sylvia Potter, who was determined to be as cooperative as she could be with the new minister.

What Is the Reception?

"The next question," replied Don, "is, What if it works? What if we do increase the number of first-time visitors? What kind of reception will a stranger receive here?"

"That's not our concern," retorted Amos Verhoef. "That's not our committee's responsibility. That's up to the ushers. All we do is call on visitors who want to be called on."

"No, that is part of our responsibility," corrected Sylvia in a none-too-gentle tone of voice. "What kind of questions should we be asking ourselves as we explore that issue?"

"In general terms," explained Don, glad for the chance to pursue the point, "we need to ask, What is the atmosphere? Do our people greet strangers? Will several of our members make the effort to become friends with the visitor? Who will secure the visitor's name and address? Will someone invite the stranger out for the noon meal?

"Just the other day I read somewhere," continued Pastor

Johnson, "that on any given Sunday more than one-half of all visitors in Protestant churches on this continent worshipped with the congregation at least once previously during the past two months. What brought them back? What does our church do to invite visitors to return? Do we invite them to come again? Will someone from this committee make a personal visit on them by Tuesday evening?

"In seminary I was told," continued Don, "the most influential question that can be asked of a first-time visitor is, 'Would you like to come home with us for dinner?' Does anyone here ask that question of first-time visitors?"

"That's an excellent idea!" exclaimed Florence Meyer, a forty-five-year-old gregarious individual. "Why don't we have one member of our committee scheduled each Sunday to ask visitors to come home with them for the noon meal? I can see that would make a great impression on a stranger."

"If you're serious about that, Florence, we're going to have to enlarge our committee and replace some of the present members," declared Ian MacGregor. "My wife would kill me if I invited a family of strangers to come home with us for Sunday dinner."

"Allow me to make one more observation on this point," continued Don. "We must remember that every visitor to our church has a reason for coming. They did not drop in simply to kill time! If we can discover why they came, we have taken the most important single step in being able to respond effectively to their needs! Discovering this reason usually requires more than a polite, 'Good morning.' Who will do this in our congregation? The greeters? The ushers? The minister? Members of the evangelism committee? Who?"

"You're the minister," replied Amos Verhoef. "Why can't you do that? Wouldn't that be the simplest way? When you greet the visitors at the door as they leave after the service, couldn't you ask them why they came?"

"It's not quite as simple as that," explained Don, silently wondering why Amos had been elected to this committee. "We need a redundant system. For example, if a visitor goes out another door and I miss them, we need a back-up system to make sure they are greeted and welcomed and that someone remembers their name.

"Before we go into this any further," continued Don, as he decided that part of his job that evening was to help some of the members of the evangelism committee learn more about contemporary reality, "there are three changes that have taken place in our society in recent years that should be a part of our strategy for attracting more visitors.

"First of all," he explained, "a great many more people now shop for a church. They no longer automatically go to the church closest to their place of residence when they move into a new community nor do they automatically pick a church from their own denominational family. That means we must make a greater effort to reach and attract those church shoppers.

"The second change is the tremendous increase in the number of marriages in which the partners come from two different religious backgrounds. The number of Catholic-Protestant marriages has more than doubled since 1950. As people marry later in life, they are more likely to meet their future spouse at work or on some recreational occasion rather than in college. The Lutheran who marries a Baptist may go to a Methodist church after they set up housekeeping, and later on, when they move to a new community, they may end up in a Presbyterian or a Lutheran parish or a church of some other denomination. We need to place a greater emphasis on attracting people because of what we can offer to meet their needs, rather than because they have moved into this neighborhood or because they grew up in our denomination or they like the looks of our building. For example, today the average Protestant congregation can expect that somewhere between 15 and 50 percent of its next one hundred adult new members will be persons who grew up in the Catholic Church. The high percentages are for those congregations in a community in which a large proportion of the population is Catholic.

"The third change we should be conscious of is the record number of women who are giving birth to their first child," concluded Don. "In 1957 a total of slightly less than 1.2 million

American women gave birth to their first child. In 1985, despite the fact that a half million fewer babies were born that year than in 1957, approximately 1.5 million women gave birth to their first child. One out of ten of these was past thirty when her first baby arrived, compared to one in twenty-five in 1970. That suggests we need to be especially concerned about reaching those families in which both the husband and wife dropped out of church when they were teenagers, but now that these couples have a baby or two, a great many of them are looking to return to church."

"What are you suggesting we do?" asked one member of the committee. "In terms of a specific plan of action, what do you think we should do?"

"We might consider a two-part approach," replied Pastor Johnson. "One part would be a series of efforts to attract people other than on Sunday morning. The second part, which we could work at concurrently, would be to review our overall effort to attract visitors to Sunday morning worship. I think it might be wise to appoint three task forces, one to plan what we could do on Christmas Eve, one to look into the possibility of creating a Mother's Club, and the third to review our efforts to attract more visitors on Sunday morning."

Christmas Eve

From an evangelistic perspective, perhaps the most significant development of recent years is that, for many people born back in the two decades following the end of World War II, who either never attended church or who dropped out as teenagers, Christmas Eve has turned out to be the most attractive and inviting re-entry point to come back into the fellowship of a worshipping community.

An increasing number of congregations are responding to this trend by inviting everyone in the community (via the local newspaper or direct mailing to every household in the area or radio spots or all three) to "come worship with us on Christmas Eve if you do not have a church home in this community." Today it is not unusual to hear a pastor comment, "Our attendance on Christmas Eve was twice what it averages through the rest of the year," or, "Our Christmas Eve attendance now exceeds our Easter attendance because so many of our members go away for a week when school is out for spring vacation," or, "Close to half of the people who show up here on Christmas Eve are not from member families."

A significant number of parents and grandparents will urge that the number-one client should be the children. They encourage planning a service that is oriented to children and may include an active role for many children.

In at least a few churches the evangelism committee, not the worship committee, carries the basic responsibility for planning the Christmas Eve service on the premise that this is the best day of the year to reach people who do not have an active church affiliation.

Who is the number-one client for your Christmas Eve service? The answer may influence the schedule.

The Schedule

The identification of the primary client may be the first factor in planning the Christmas Eve schedule. If the goal is to fill the building or if the family reunion theme is the dominant factor, it may be wise to plan only one service. If, however, the Sunday morning attendance averages close to one hundred or more, and if the goal is to reach more people with the news that God did send His only Son into the world, it may be wise to plan two or three or more services.

One format, for example, is to schedule a "birthday party for Jesus" for very young children for late afternoon on December 24, shortly after the end of nap time. A second service, planned primarily for slightly older children and their parents, may be scheduled for 6:30 or 7:00 P.M. This service may include the children's choir. The 8:00 or 8:30 P.M. service may be built around music with the youth choir singing, and the adult choir may sing at the late service that begins around 10:00 or 11:00 P.M.

A format similar to this one may be followed in those churches that (a) are seeking to reach unchurched families with very young children, (b) want to offer everyone meaningful choices, (c) expect the attendance will be two or three times what it was on the average Sunday morning in October, (d) desire to include two or three or four choirs, but do not expect one choir to sing more than once on Christmas Eve, (e) plan to take advantage of the trend that Christmas Eve has become a major re-entry point into the church for young adults who dropped out a decade or more ago, (f) are organized to greet and welcome first-time visitors at each service, (g) have a system for following up on first-time visitors to invite them to return, (h) are prepared to invest money in advertising to invite nonmembers to attend, (i) have the capability to plan at least three or four months in advance, (j) do not include in policy-making positions more than one or two influential leaders who are more interested in having a huge crowd at one service than in reaching more people, (k) assume some members will attend two or three services, (l) are convinced much of what happens in this world is the result of creating the self-fulfilling prophecy, and (m) are optimistic about December weather.

Mothers' Club

At least eight reasons can be offered to explain the remarkable increase in the number of Mothers' Clubs that have emerged across the continent in recent years. These include (1) the record number of women giving birth to their first child (in 1985, 43 percent of all babies were firstborns compared to 26 percent in 1961) and the normal anxiety mothers feel about that first baby, (2) the research that suggests postpartem depression is far less common among new mothers who are part of a continuing mutual support group, (3) the tremendous surge of interest in serious daytime Bible study among the generation born after 1955, (4) the sharp increase in the number of mothers giving birth to their child after several years of full-time employment (the number of women age twenty-five and over when they gave birth to their first child increased from 269,000 in 1970 to nearly 600,000 in 1985), many of whom need to build a new circle of friends when they leave the labor force to become homemakers, (5) the increase in the number of single-parent mothers (from 2.9 million in 1970 to over 6 million in 1985) who feel a need for a mutual support group, (6) the growing interest in the whole subject of parenting, especially among first-time parents, (7) the growing number of young parents who do not live in the same state in which either set of their parents resides, and (8) the growing number of congregations who are serious in their efforts to attract this new generation of young parents by focussing on the needs of these people rather than on trying to fill empty pews.

Mothers' Clubs take many different forms. Some meet weekly, more meet once or twice a month. A few are directed solely at that rapidly growing number of women who give birth by a C-section procedure. One meets Monday, Wednesday, and Friday for (a) an aerobic dance class, (b) fellowship, mutual support, sharing, and lunch, and (c) an after-lunch hour with a specialist on some phase of parenting. The host church offers a free baby-sitting service for this four-hour period. Another meets weekly as a combination Bible study–mutual support–fellowship group. In another congregation the Mothers' Club meets every Tuesday evening with baby-sitting provided by the host church, and three-quarters of the participants are single parent mothers. In hundreds of congregations, the Mothers' Club is a circle in the women's organization for mothers of preschool children and meets monthly.

In many of these the key to continuity is the mature grandmother who officially is the "sponsor" or "adviser" or "staff representative" and who fills the roles of confidante, organizer, executive secretary, respected older adult, surrogate mother, keeper of the calendar, teacher, friend, gadfly, glue, counsellor, and membership secretary.

Pastor Don Johnson was correct in placing a high priority on the need to make St. John's a more attractive and inviting place for first-time visitors. He also offered the committee a useful analysis of the changes in our society that have produced a sharp increase in the number of church shoppers. His suggestions for a two-part strategy, with a special emphasis on special events and narrowly focussed groups, such as a Mothers' Club, also were relevant proposals.

In addition, however, there are four other facets of a larger strategy that should be considered by the leaders of any congregation who are interested in attracting more visitors.

Are Your Members Inviting People?

The first, and by far the most influential, factor in determining whether a congregation has a great many or few visitors can be found in the attitudes and actions of the members.

Some families have many guests. Others have very few. The big difference is some families invite others to come to their home while others do not. The same is true in the church. Some congregations have scores of visitors every week because many of the members invite friends, neighbors, business acquaintances, relatives, and newcomers to come to church with them. In other churches this rarely happens. What is the difference?

Basically there are six differences. Congregations in which the members invite others to come to church with them usually display these characteristics: (a) the members are enthusiastic about their faith as Christians, (b) the members are enthusiastic about their congregation, (c) the members are enthusiastic about the *current* pastor, (d) the congregation as a whole conveys the expectation that members will invite others to come to church with them, (e) most of the members actively and enthusiastically greet and welcome visitors, and (f) a particular program or, if it is on Sunday morning, a worship experience, is planned on the assumption that first-time visitors will be present—which means minimizing references to "last week," to congregational problems, to administrative concerns, or to "in house" jokes that leave the stranger mystified.

Obviously there are scores of growing communities where these factors can be ignored and the turnover in the population will produce a reliable flow of visitors, but those are the exceptions. Most churches do not enjoy the benefits of that kind of community setting.

Do You Advertise?

The second most influential factor in attracting visitors that was not discussed at the meeting at St. John's is advertising. Every church has control over how it will advertise itself. Congregations that are seriously interested in attracting visitors often allocate at least 5 percent of the operating budget for advertising and public relations. In broad general terms the most cost effective advertising channels for a majority of congregations are, in this order, (1) a sign or bulletin board in front of the building, (2) a telephone with the church's name listed in the telephone directory, (3) an advertisement in the Yellow Pages with instructions on how to find the building, (4) a direct-mail invitation to every household in the community that specifically invites nonmembers to a special event or program such as at Christmas Eve or a workshop on step-parenting or a new ministry with parents who have experienced the death of a son or daughter or a divorce recovery program or a film series on parenting, (5) a series of thirty to fifty 30-second spots on the local radio station that services that slice of the population you are seeking to reach, (6) a series of display advertisements in the local newspaper, preferably on Monday or Tuesday, but definitely not on Friday or Saturday, (7) a weekly ad in the shopping "throw-away" that is delivered to every home in your community, and (8) cable television—in hundreds of smaller communities, however, cable television may be the second or third most cost-effective advertising channel.

There are several books on the market that can be useful in designing your advertising campaign.[1] Be sure to recognize the values of repetition and of targeting a precisely defined audience. Frequently this will mean inviting strangers to a particular program such as a Mothers' Club that meets every Tuesday or your Christmas Eve service or a series of special programs for parents of teenagers. You may receive a larger response to promotional efforts that invite people to special events than you receive from advertising the Sunday morning service.

What Is the Community Image?

By far the most subtle of any of these approaches to attracting first-time visitors is the community image of your church. The congregations that project the clearest image of who and what they are tend to be the churches that have the largest number of visitors. This image may reflect a particular program, such as the ministry of music or the youth group or Bible study classes or the preaching or the weekday nursery school or the ministry with mature adults. Or, it may reflect more subjective characteristics such as a "caring congregation" or "an exciting church" or a "friendly parish" or a "youthful congregation." What is the image your congregation projects to the community? Is it one that will attract visitors? Can you reinforce the image you want to project?

Who Is the Pastor?

While this last factor is more popular with the laity than the clergy, it is an indisputable fact that some pastors attract visitors while others do not. The ones who attract the most visitors are the ministers who have been given permission by the congregation to spend considerable time calling in the homes of unchurched persons and prospective new members.

The next group of pastors who attract visitors are those who spend considerable time as highly visible community leaders, who serve in the local volunteer fire department, who are active in a local service club, or who broadcast over radio or who appear frequently on a local cable television channel or both.

The third group of pastors who personally are responsible for many visitors in a typical year are those who have been serving the same congregation for two or three decades or longer. When this long tenure is combined with an earned reputation as a superb preacher, that almost always results in an above average number of visitors.

A distant fourth group is the colorful and magnetic personality who draws visitors in the same way a light bulb on the front porch attracts moths at night. While this category has tremendous visibility, it is doubtful if there are as many as three hundred of these ministers on the North American continent. The vast majority of ministers who personally attract visitors fit into one or more of the first three categories. The pastor who attracts the most visitors typically has been serving that congregation for at least a decade, is an excellent preacher, rarely calls on members except in emergencies, stays away from most committee and board meetings, neglects his or her family, is not active in denominational or ecumenical affairs, and makes at least five hundred calls a year on nonmembers. Few congregations are willing to pay that price for more visitors.

What is the strategy your congregation follows to attract more visitors?

THIRTEEN

RESTAURANT OR CHURCH?

Reverend, we've been behind you and supported you in everything you've asked us to do for seven years," declared Marge Hopkins as she cornered Pastor Don Johnson when he was coming out of the post office one sunny Tuesday morning. "The time has come for you to go to bat for us and you know what we want. We want a new kitchen in that new fellowship hall! The idea of asking us to prepare meals in that old kitchen in the basement of the old building, put them on a cart, and wheel them all the way over to the new hall is absolute nonsense and we won't stand for it!"

Two years earlier everyone at St. John's Church agreed that the time had come to construct an addition to the thirty-three-year-old building that housed the congregation. The membership had grown to the point that more space was needed. Perhaps even more influential was the fact that in the seven years since Don had arrived on the scene as the new pastor, morale was up, worship attendance was up, the level of member giving had more than doubled, the program had been expanded, three part-time lay-program staff members had been added, the pace of congregational life had accelerated, the median age of the membership was dropping, and enthusiasm and optimism had never been greater. One result was that every year the old fellowship hall in the basement

142

looked smaller, less inviting, more out-of-date, and less adequate.

The terrain was such that people could continue to enter the sanctuary from the street level, but the proposed addition in the rear would be on the same level as the parking lot and the floor of the basement. Thus those who were coming to worship could walk into the sanctuary from the street without climbing stairs while those who parked in the rear could enter the new wing without climbing any stairs. The proposal for the new one-story building included a large fellowship hall, a kitchen, four classrooms, and two restrooms. The old fellowship hall would be remodeled into classrooms, and three of the first-floor classrooms in the original building would be remodeled into an office area as part of the second stage of the total project.

Unfortunately, when the bids had been opened a few days earlier, the lowest bid was $30,800 above the architect's estimate.

The previous evening the building committee had met to decide on how to respond to that unpleasant surprise. One proposal was to go ahead with the lowest bid, even though this would mean postponing the renovations called for in the second stage by at least three or four years.

When this failed to arouse unanimous support, Dick Baker urged, "The simplest place to cut back would be to eliminate the kitchen. By turning that space into another classroom we can save at least $30,000. We really don't need a big new kitchen. We can use the old kitchen in the old section whenever we need a stove or a sink. I talked with the architect yesterday and he agreed this change will save us close to $30,000 and we'll get one more classroom. That's a bargain if I ever heard of one!"

"I'll second that motion," chimed in Bill Michell. "If we can save $30,000 by taking the kitchen out of the plans, that will enable us to go ahead with the lowest bid. It would be more economical to cater the meals. Twelve percent interest on $30,000 figures out to $300 a month, and you can hire a lot of catering for $3,600 a year!"

That same evening in a different congregation in another

state six women were busy in the kitchen preparing to serve the quarterly congregational dinner. "They told me yesterday to prepare for one hundred and fifty," commented one of the women, "and now it looks as if we're going to have over two hundred. It seems that the only time our people come out is when we feed them."

"Sometimes I wonder whether this is a church or a restaurant," questioned another of the harried workers.

For the Reverend Don Johnson at St. John's Church, the debate over whether or not the new building should include a spacious and expensive kitchen was not the basic issue. That was simply the form in which a divisive political issue was being debated. A classic definition of a political issue is the allocation of scarce resources among competing demands. At St. John's the current scarcity was dollars for the building program. Should $30,000 of that scarce resource be allocated to a new kitchen? Should Don side with Marge Hopkins and other leaders in the women's organization at St. John's? Or should he support the point of view of Dick Baker, Bill Michell, and others who opposed that expenditure?

How important is the kitchen? Is it really worth all it costs? Should a church serve meals, or is that unfair competition with taxpaying public facilities? Is it realistic in today's world to expect volunteers to staff the kitchen? Would it not be simpler for everyone to eat at home before they come to the meeting at the church rather than carry all that food in and have to carry all the dishes and pans back home?

These are only a few of the questions and objections raised by those who display little sympathy for that elaborate, but sometimes rarely used, church kitchen. Rather than attempt to respond to these objections, it might be better to begin with two assumptions and a question.

First, churches differ greatly from one another and it would be presumptuous to suggest that the same response will be appropriate for all types and sizes of congregations on such a controversial issue as the value of church kitchens.

Second, some churches will find a kitchen to be of greater value than others.

Finally, we come to the central question: Which congregations are most likely to benefit from a kitchen in the church and why?

The Small Church

The small congregation that averages fewer than one hundred at worship on Sunday morning often resembles a family. Three out of five of all the Protestant congregations on the North American continent fit into this bracket. Since this is the most common size of church, it deserves to be discussed first.

If one thinks of these congregations as a very large or extended family, it is easier to understand the need for a kitchen. Just as every family feels a need for its own kitchen, even those living in one-room apartments, so these smaller churches need a kitchen.

When the clan gathers, the feeling of kinship and fellowship is enhanced when we eat together. The occasion may be the meal before the annual meeting or following the graveside services for a deceased member of the clan or the Sunday school picnic or the annual celebration of the anniversary of the founding of that congregation or the gathering to celebrate the conclusion of vacation Bible school or the reception for the new minister or the celebration of one couple's fiftieth wedding anniversary. Each one is a family reunion, and when the family gets together, we eat together! Eating together is one of the most effective means of reinforcing family ties.

This strongly relational dimension of the small membership church is the basic reason that there is a kitchen in nearly every building housing this size and type of congregation. The family needs it!

The Middle-sized Church

For purposes of this discussion, the middle-sized congregation averages between one hundred and two hundred at Sunday morning worship. One Protestant congregation out of four on this continent fits into this category. While some of the smaller congregations in this bracket act much like overgrown small churches, most of them are far more complex, and the debate over the value of a kitchen must take into account this complexity.

The kitchen in the middle-sized church should be seen as a reinforcement for the ongoing program of that congregation. Eating together usually does not resemble the family reunion as it does in the small membership church. In the middle-sized church those who gather to eat together usually reflect a particular slice of the total program and ministry of that congregation.

Examples of this include the monthly dinner party by that big adult Sunday school class that schedules eleven social events every year, or the dinner that is a part of the first training session for those who signed up to be callers in the annual visitation-evangelism program, or the Sweethearts' Dinner scheduled every February by the Men's Fellowship to which wives or girlfriends are invited, or the special breakfast one Sunday morning honoring the teachers in the Sunday school, or the meal served for the annual meeting of the women's organization at which officers will be elected for the new year, or the meal served at 5:30 every Wednesday afternoon to the children and adult leadership of the youth club.

Each of these events share several common characteristics: (a) the gathering or program is planned for only a fraction of the total membership, sometimes as few as 3 or 4 or 5 percent, not for the whole family, (b) the meal is a significant component of the particular program or gathering, (c) those in charge have learned that elimination of the meal will result in a lower attendance, (d) eating together is not the reason for gathering, but it is a reinforcement for what is planned to happen when those folks gather and, perhaps most important of all, (e) the meal reinforces the ties of newcomers to the particular group, class, organization, or choir.

In other words, the kitchen can be a very useful tool for strengthening the cohesiveness of group life and for the specialized programs and ministries of the middle-sized congregation.

The Large Church

Perhaps the critical part of the context for examining the place of the kitchen in large churches is that most of these really are congregations of congregations. Many of the churches averaging more than two hundred at Sunday morning worship offer two or three or more worship services every weekend. This means those "regulars" who come to the early service on Sunday morning rarely see the "regulars" who attend the late service. In other large churches the real division is between the oldtimers, who are on a first-name basis with one another, and the newcomers, who appear to be an anonymous part of the passing parade to most of the longtime members.

To many members the large congregation really is a conglomeration of the various groups, classes, circles, organizations, choirs, cells, and fellowships, which is held together by corporate worship experiences, the paid staff, the name, the weekly newsletter, and perhaps a common goal or two. Yet the primary loyalty of scores of members is to that small face-to-face group. That is where they have gained a sense of belonging. That is where they know they will be missed if they are absent.

That is the context for evaluating the role of the church kitchen. The primary value of the church kitchen in the large church is to facilitate those large group events and gatherings that bring two or three hundred or more people together across those lines that represent the compartmentalization of the large congregation. This means scheduling somewhere between eight and three dozen large group events every year that will bring together people from the various subcongregations that constitute the large church.

Before looking for examples of this kind of gathering, a word needs to be said about a few of the common characteristics of the large group event that brings together two hundred or more people. Five stand out for our attention in this discussion. Most large group programs that represent occasional, as contrasted with regular, gatherings depend heavily on (a) a carefully planned schedule and program, (b) food, (c) humor and laughter, (d) a physical focal point for gathering people's attention, and (e) music. Football games, political conventions, the annual denominational meeting, and the annual regional training school for people in Christian education in the churches can be cited to illustrate the importance of all five components. In the large church the fellowship hall needs a stage, a piano, and a nearby kitchen.

Examples of these large group gatherings that cut across the compartmental lines include the breakfast for those sharing in the Easter sunrise service; the long New Year's Eve program that begins with a color slide review of the year now ending, shifts over to the watchnight service, and concludes with a party; the annual school of religion for six consecutive weeks; the Wednesday evening package that begins with a meal and includes a variety of other events ranging from the weekly rehearsal for the children's choir to an adult Bible study group; the annual dinner celebrating the founding of the congregation; the special program celebrating the twenty-fifth anniversary of the senior minister's ordination; the hanging of the greens ceremony in the late afternoon and evening of the first Sunday of Advent; the dinner at which a national official of the denomination will be the speaker; the spaghetti supper sponsored by the high school youth to raise money for their summer work camp trip; and the annual event that recognizes and honors those members retiring from positions of major leadership responsibility in the congregation.

In the large churches the kitchen is a useful tool for bringing people together from those "subcongregations." It also, of course, will be used to reinforce a variety of specialized programs similar to what takes place in the middle-sized church.

A secondary value of the kitchen in those large congregations that are confronted with a shortage of space is to begin earlier on Sunday morning, with breakfast. One church offers breakfast at 7:30 in the morning followed by worship at 8:00,

9:30, and 11:00. Breakfast increases the size of the crowd at the first service. Several congregations offer worship at 8:00 on Sunday morning followed by breakfast at 9:00. Others offer an early "adult class at breakfast" at 7:30 Sunday morning, followed by worship at 8:30 or 9:00.

Who Staffs It?

When the question is raised about who will work in the kitchen or who will take care of it, four generalizations emerge.

In the small membership churches, members of the family will look after the kitchen. Naturally this can be seen most clearly in ethnic and nationality congregations.

In the middle-sized churches, it usually is necessary and appropriate to have a committee responsible for the kitchen.

In the larger churches with a modest level of weekday programming, it often is useful to have a committee provide for the staffing and care of the kitchen, but frequently this does not work. As a result staffing often is a continuing problem in these congregations.

In the larger churches with an extensive program, much of which is dependent on use of the kitchen, the load usually is too much to expect volunteers to carry. An occasional solution is provided by the woman who enlists and organizes a large group of volunteers to carry the complete load, but without overloading anyone except the person in charge. More often the church secretary or the director of Christian education or some other paid staff member voluntarily picks up this assignment. The growing trend, especially in the very large congregations in the South with an extensive program, is to add to the paid staff, often on a part-time basis, a person who will have responsibility for the general oversight of the kitchen, including the enlistment of volunteers.

Four Concluding Comments

As you reflect on the role of the kitchen in your church, please keep in mind four other facets of this issue.

First, be careful not to let a means-to-an-end become an end in itself. A kitchen is justifiable only if used as a part of the ministry of the congregation. Keeping it locked up to protect it with the result it rarely is utilized is almost equivalent to creating false idols.

Second, a kitchen can offer many fringe benefits ranging from opportunities to express creative skills (some people express their creativity through their hands rather than through words) to the assimilation of new members to opening another door for active male participation.

Third, reflect on these four observations. The members most likely to "drop out" of church are those who do not have any close friends in the congregation. Those least likely to drop out are members who have five or more close friends in the congregation. One of the most effective means of developing close friendships is to work closely with someone else on a common task. The most widely used method of reinforcing friendship ties in our society is for people to eat together.

Perhaps the kitchen can be a valuable tool in reducing the dropout rate in your congregation.

Finally, those who question the place or importance of eating may benefit from a visit to a new shopping mall. A dozen years ago nearly every enclosed mall barred fast-food places or any dining facility except the most expensive restaurants. Today's new generation of shopping malls may have as many as a dozen fast-food operations on the perimeter of a common area filled with tables, chairs, and benches. This new look is part of an effort to create a family atmosphere to replace the old concept that the mall catered to individual shoppers. That may say something to those congregations seeking to enhance their images as a family church. It also may influence the discussions in your congregation about the value of a church kitchen.

FOURTEEN

THE ODDS
IN MINISTRY

N ext week I have five weddings," commented Pastor Johnson to his friend Professor Walter Roberts, who taught sociology at the local community college and was a close personal friend of Don's, as well as an active parishioner and loyal ally. "That's the most I've ever had in one week in all my years in the pastorate."

"Naturally," observed Professor Roberts, "for every three marriages in 1960 there will be five this year. You should be officiating at more weddings now than ever before in your ministry!"

"Yes, but aren't a lot of people choosing a civil ceremony now, rather than a church wedding?"

"Depends on where you live," came the reply. "In Georgia, where we lived before moving here, less than one-half (44 percent) of the women getting married for the first time had a religious ceremony. Here in Indiana nine out of ten women being married for the first time chose a church wedding. The only place you could go where that percentage would be higher would be West Virginia, where the proportion is 98 percent."

"That's two reasons, I guess, why I'm having more weddings now," reflected Pastor Johnson. "What else can you tell me?"

"Well, first of all, you should expect to have four times as many weddings here in Indiana every year as you did twenty years ago when you began your ministry in South Carolina," came the reply.

"Second, you can expect that three-quarters of your weddings will be either on Friday or Saturday. Tuesday and Wednesday together account for only one wedding out of eleven.

"Third, as you probably know from experience, June is the month with the most weddings, followed by July, May, and August. January has the fewest with about half as many weddings as June, and February has the second smallest number of weddings.

"Fourth, if you have five weddings scheduled for next week, that means ten people will be getting married. On an overall average you could expect six or seven of the ten will be getting married for the first time. However, since these are all religious ceremonies that figure will be a little higher. When the bride is getting married for the second time, only 60 percent of those weddings are religious ceremonies. Therefore I would guess that eight of the ten will be getting married for the first time."

"You're exactly right," replied Don. "Now let's see if you can tell me what will happen to these marriages. How many will end in divorce?"

"No one can answer that question now," replied the statistically minded professor. "Contrary to what we read—that half of today's marriages will end in divorce—we simply do not have enough experience with the marriages being performed this year to be absolutely certain what will happen.

"Back in November, 1980, the National Center for Health Statistics published a study they had made of marriages contracted in 1952, 1962, and 1972. They found that 29 percent of the marriages of 1952—that was twenty-five years earlier—already had ended in divorce. They estimated that another 3 percent or so of those 1952 marriages also would be terminated by divorce."

"That's a lot lower percentage than the figures I keep reading," interrupted Pastor Johnson. "If I understand correctly, you're saying that one-third of the marriages of 1952 will end in divorce and two-thirds will be terminated by death?"

"Correct," came the reply. "But let me complete my statement. That same study predicted that 40 percent of the marriages entered into in 1962 would end in divorce. And nearly 20 percent of the marriages contracted in 1972 already had ended in divorce by 1977. The study predicted that 49 percent of the 1977 marriages would end in divorce."

"That's a more pessimistic set of figures," observed Don. "That does suggest that about one-half of today's marriages do end in divorce."

"To be more precise," continued his friend, "that study predicted that of the 2.2 million marriages entered into in 1977, one-fifth would be terminated by divorce within five years and another one-fifth would be divorced by the end of fifteen years. If those patterns prevail for the five weddings you will perform next week, that means one couple will be divorced within five years and another couple will be divorced some time between the fifth and fifteenth year of their marriage."

"Do you think I should revise the ritual to include those predictions?" asked Pastor Johnson with a smile.

"No, but you may be reassured by the fact that a significantly smaller proportion of church weddings end in divorce than is the case with civil ceremonies. You also should note," added the friend, "there is a correlation between age at marriage and divorce. The younger the age of the couple getting married, the greater the chance of divorce.

"During the past several years the median age at first marriage has gone up substantially. For men it is now higher than it has been since 1900. For women the median age at first marriage in 1984 was 23.3 years and it was 25.4 years for men. That means one-half of the women getting married for the first time in 1984 were more than twenty-three years of age. That's the highest it has ever been in American history. That may produce a decline in the divorce rate and that may be one reason why the number of divorces has been declining in recent years.

"Before we leave this subject of marriage and divorce," continued Professor Roberts, "you may be interested to know that one of the most remarkable examples of continuity in American family life during the past 150 years has been in the dissolution rate of marriages. With only four major exceptions the proportion of marriages terminated by death or divorce each year has fluctuated in the narrow range of 2.8 percent to 3.5 percent. One exception was the Civil War era when the rate climbed to 3.8 percent. A second was in 1918–19 when the combination of a modest increase in the divorce rate following the end of World War I plus the influenza epidemic of 1918–19 caused the end of 4 percent of all marriages in a twelve month period. The third exception was in 1946 when the number of divorces jumped by a third over the average for that era and 3.7 percent of all marriages were terminated that year. The fourth exception began in the early 1970s when the number of marriages ending in divorce each year climbed from 700,000 in 1970 to over a million in 1975 to nearly 1.2 million annually in recent years. In 1985, 4 percent of all marriages were ended by death or divorce.

"Since 1975 slightly more than one-half of the marriages that came to an end in any one year were dissolved by divorce. That is unprecedented in American history; even back in 1946 when divorces reached a new record high of 610,000, more marriages were dissolved by death than by divorce. As recently as 1964, death was the cause of more than 60 percent of all marriages dissolved that year. By contrast, in 1985 death terminated 45 percent of all marriages that were dissolved compared to the 1.2 million or 55 percent that ended in divorce."

"What else do you have in your bag of statistical tricks that will help me better understand this parish and my ministry?" inquired Pastor Johnson.

"Well, first of all, I believe you reported exactly 500 confirmed members at the end of last year," observed the friend in changing the subject. "If your members represent a cross section of the American population, that means your parish includes six or seven members who no longer would be alive if the national death rate had remained unchanged since 1970. You've had five fewer funerals during the past several years because of the advances made by medical science in keeping people alive."

"I find that a little hard to believe," replied Pastor Johnson.

"In the years I've been here our confirmed membership has hovered very close to 500, some years a little higher and some years a little lower, but we've averaged nine member-deaths a year and each of the last two years was exactly nine. How do you explain that?"

"That suggests either that your members as a whole are older than the American population, or else you have a lot of poor drivers in this parish," came the reply. "In most of the mainline denominations a congregation of 500 confirmed members could expect to average six member deaths a year. If you average nine, that suggests your members are significantly older than the membership of the denomination as a whole.

"For Lutherans, for example, the death rate was 11.85 per 1,000 confirmed members in 1982, down from 12.08 in 1972. This was a substantially smaller decline than was true for the American population as a whole. If this is an older than average group of people, you probably have eight or ten members who are still alive today due to the medical advances achieved since 1970. For example, a denomination with one million members probably has slightly more than 10,000 more confirmed members today than it would have had if these medical breakthroughs had not been achieved. For the nation as a whole there are three million people still alive who would not be alive without that remarkable drop in the death rate."

"If I remember correctly some things I've read elsewhere," observed Betty White, who had been sitting and listening silently for several minutes, "one of the reasons for the increase in the divorce rate and in the number of people dying of cancer is that people are living longer."

"That's correct," agreed Walter Roberts. "For every person who dies from tuberculosis this year, forty died from the same cause back in 1900. People have to die of something some time, so as fewer die from the traditional diseases, more live long enough to die from cancer. Likewise some marriages that once would have been terminated by the death of one spouse now end in divorce.

"Furthermore," continued Professor Roberts, "the increase in the life expectancy of mature adults has had a profound impact on our society. This ranges from an increase in the number of people in nursing homes to slowing the rate of membership decline in several denominations such as the Methodists, Presbyterians, and Disciples, to the sharp increase in the number of people with Alzheimer's disease, and the increase in the number of adult day care centers."

"Some of those are hopeful trends, if I understand what you're saying," offered Pastor Johnson. "You're telling us that a significant factor in church growth is that people are living longer. My impression is that older people are more likely than younger persons to be at worship and therefore this should have a favorable impact on church attendance."

"That's correct," came the reply. "According to the Princeton Religious Research Center, 62 percent of the church members age sixty-five and over said they had attended worship within the past week, compared to 49 percent of those church members in the twenty-five to twenty-nine age bracket. In other words, if all of your 500 confirmed members are past sixty-five you could expect to have over 300 in church on an average Sunday. But if all of your members are young adults, your attendance would be under 250."

"That sure shoots holes in all the alibis I hear, which conclude that our attendance is so low because we have so many elderly members," reflected Don.

"May I change the subject?" asked Betty White. "Last spring I went to the thirtieth reunion of my college graduating class. If you're so good at figures, tell me, Walter, how many of my fellow graduates of thirty years showed up?"

"I haven't the faintest idea of what your attendance was," came the reply, "but we can tell you three or four things about your class. For example, eleven out of twelve of the graduates of thirty years ago should still be alive. Nineteen out of twenty of the women in your college graduating class of 1956 married at least once, and nine out of ten of those who married are mothers. As I pointed out earlier, nearly a third of those who had married were divorced. But most of the divorced men in your graduating class have remarried, compared to only about half of the divorced women. You also may be interested to know that half of all the marriages that took place in the late 1940s and early 1950s lasted for thirty-five years or longer and half were terminated by death or divorce before that couple could celebrate their thirty-fifth anniversary."

"Well, I guess my husband and I are part of the lucky majority," reflected Betty White. "We are both alive and still married and expect we'll make it to well past our thirty-fifth anniversary. Now, let's go back to church growth. Did I hear you suggest the way to have a numerically growing congregation is to concentrate on older adults?"

"That's not what I said," corrected the statistically oriented professor. "All I said was that folks are living longer and that church attendance correlates with age. Since the number of mature adults in our population is increasing, one approach to church growth would be to concentrate your evangelistic outreach on older people who are not active in any church. The number of Americans age sixty-five and older *doubled* in thirty years, from a little over 12 million in 1950 to 25 million in 1980. And this group is expected to reach 32 million by the year 2000.

"An alternative would be to concentrate on the newly married. The number of marriages in the United States peaked (percentage-wise) at nearly 2.3 million in 1946, dropped to 1.5 million in the mid-1950s, and has been running at between 2.4 and 2.5 million for each of the past several years.

"Another alternative would be to focus your efforts on single parent families. That group accounted for all of the increase in the number of families with children under eighteen at home during the 1969 to 1982 period. There has been an actual decrease in the number of husband-wife couples with children under eighteen at home during the past dozen years. Few churches have a strong ministry with single parent families.

"A third alternative would be to place a higher priority on a ministry with recently remarried people. As I tried to explain to you when we began this conversation, the number of brides who are in their second or subsequent marriage has more than tripled since 1960."

"I have to leave now to make some hospital calls," declared Pastor Johnson as he looked at the clock. "Do you have any other statistical gems to help us understand what's going on in this parish?"

"Well, first of all, if you want to test your opinion that this is an aging parish, you might want to make a couple of simple checks," suggested the friend. "In 1983, for the first time in American history, Americans age sixty-five and over outnumbered teenagers. Back in 1900 there were three times as many teenagers as there were people age sixty-five and older. You might ask what the ratio is here.

"Another yardstick you can use is that in 1960 for every ten children under age five there were only eight persons age sixty-five and over. By 1980 that had changed to sixteen mature adults for every ten young children under the age of five. If you're thinking of a new building program, that's something to keep in mind. What's the ratio here today? What was it ten years ago?

"If you make ten visits to patients in the hospital, you can expect, on the average, that six will be on women and four on men. Two out of the ten visits will be with persons sixty-five or older. You also can expect to see one out of six women in your parish, and one out of ten of your male parishioners, go to the hospital some time during the next twelve months.

"One of the more ironic patterns," continued Professor Roberts, "is that on the basis of data gathered by the National Survey of Family Growth, April is by far what people see as the best month for a baby to arrive, with August, September, January, and February ranked as the least desirable. In point of fact, however, fewer babies are born in April than any other month while late summer and early fall represent the peak period for births. More than a quarter of your visits, Don, on a new mother will be in the months of July, August, and October, while only 22 percent of all babies are born in January, February, and April combined. As you may already know, approximately one birth in a hundred produces twins or triplets.

"Back in 1970 more than four out of five women giving birth to a child for the first time were under twenty-five years of age. That dropped to two out of three by 1979. In 1970 only 4 percent of all new mothers were over thirty years of age. Now nearly 10 percent of all new mothers are past thirty. So you'll be seeing more older women giving birth to their first child than you saw twenty years ago.

"The big change, however, which only the older pastors remember, is that back in 1940 only 56 percent of all babies were delivered by a physician in a hospital. Jimmy Carter was the first President of the United States to have been born in a hospital. By 1950, nine out of ten babies were born in a hospital, and today it is ninety-seven out of one hundred. One of the big positive changes is that as recently as 1940 a mother was more than forty times as likely to die in childbirth than is the case today.

"If you get a call that a teenager in your parish has died or been killed in an accident, the chances are three out of four it will be a boy.

"If an adult in your parish dies, the chances are one out of three the cause will be cancer; and three out of five deaths from cancer come to people past sixty-five years of age. As Betty mentioned earlier, the biggest single factor in the increase in deaths from cancer is that people are living longer. Fifty years ago they were more likely to die from some other cause before they developed cancer. The death rate from cancer today is twice what it was in 1940.

"If one of your members is killed in an automobile accident, the chances are nearly three out of four the victim will be male. Likewise, three-fourths of all suicides and murder victims are men. In a given year, fifty-four out of every one hundred deaths are male.

"Those figures help you understand why eleven out of thirteen widowed persons are women. Out of the people born in the first three decades of this century who are still alive, three out of ten of the women and one out of ten of the men have been widowed at least once. While two-thirds of all of the widowed women in America are past sixty-five years of age, one-third of all widows lost their husbands before the wife's forty-fifth birthday. There are a lot more young widows out there than most people realize!"

"That's more numbers than I can absorb in one sitting," protested Pastor Johnson as he left for the hospital. "You make me feel good that my job is people, not statistics."

"That's true," retorted his friend, "but remember that statistics can help you better understand both your people and your parish."

FIFTEEN

WHAT IF
IT WORKS?

Y ou know, when he first came here, Pastor Johnson did a lot of calling on people in their homes," reflected Mrs. Anderson, "but that seems to be part of the past. It's more than two years now since he last stopped in to see me."

"I know exactly what you mean," agreed Mrs. Bradley. "If I've heard that very same comment once, I've heard it at least fifty times during the past year! Instead of calling on the members like he ought to, he's always off chasing down someone who doesn't go to church anywhere and probably never will."

"Now, please don't be too harsh," cautioned Mrs. Carter. "A minister is supposed to be looking for new members from among the unchurched. What bothers me is that last week he told the choir he was planning three services this next winter for Christmas Eve and that he expected us to be prepared to sing at all three. Two years ago, when he decided we should have two services on Christmas Eve, some of the choir rebelled. We nearly filled the church for both of them this past year, but I really can't see why we need three."

"It seems Don could honor us with his presence more than once a year," complained Bill Dempsey to the other trustees at their monthly meeting.

"Well, he's pretty busy, you know," offered Jack Edwards.

"This church has grown a lot since he came and a lot of his time is taken up with all those new members. And besides, I believe he actually did meet with us on three different occasions last year. It would help, however, if he could at least come by other than when he's got some special project he's pushing."

"We're not the only ones he's neglecting," added Ben Fuller. "Last Tuesday I was sitting next to the Methodist minister at the Lion's Club and he told me our pastor rarely attends the local ministerial meetings anymore."

These comments illustrate several of the price tags the minister usually must pay to achieve an effective church growth strategy. It may be useful to look more closely at five of these price tags on the evangelism program that works and on the response of one minister to those price tags.

"But He Never Calls"

Far and away the most common criticism by longtime members of what has become a rapidly growing congregation is that the pastor does not spend enough time calling on the members. This is what economists call a "fixed sum problem." The minister has only 168 hours in a week. Time spent on evangelism and church growth must be taken from some part of the week's schedule. The usual practice for the minister with an intentional growth strategy is to concentrate on prospective new members and hope that "next month I'll have some time to visit a few of the oldtimers." Next month, of course, never comes.

In broader terms, one of the most difficult decisions for the pastor with a strong desire to facilitate church growth is choosing between the popular alternative of spending considerable time with the members or devoting many hours every week to carrying out the new member enlistment program.

By contrast, the minister who is more oriented toward a shepherding role than toward evangelism comes to a different conclusion. "This week I must give a high priority to calling on several of our members who need attention, and next week I'll

get out and call on some of the prospective new members."
Both pastors often feel frustrated.

Unpopular Innovations

In the vast majority of congregations the implementation of
an effective church growth strategy will require an expansion of
the present program and the addition of new ministries. A
common example of that, which Don Johnson initiated at St.
John's Church, is the addition of a second or a third or fourth or
fifth service on Christmas Eve. Despite the fact this usually
results in a substantial increase in the total attendance, it often
draws complaints. "I missed some of my old friends who went
to the other service." "That's an unfair load to place on the
choir." "I liked it better when the church was packed and we
had to bring in chairs." "There were so many strangers there, I
didn't feel like I was in my own church."

The basic reason for adding another service to the Christmas
Eve schedule is not to please the members or to increase the
attendance. The basic reason for that innovation is that
Christmas Eve has emerged in many communities as the most
popular time for young parents who "dropped out of church" a
decade earlier "to come back to church." One of the
responsibilities of the minister who wants to encourage church
growth is to be able and willing to serve as an innovator, even
when some of the changes will not be universally popular.

Delegating Responsibility

The minister who has been trained to be the shepherd of the
flock, always available and always responsive to every call,
often has difficulty delegating both authority and responsibility
to individuals and groups. Every committee sees itself as one of
the two or three most important committees in the church. "We
can understand why the pastor cannot meet with every
committee, and we can understand that it would be poor
stewardship of time for the minister to meet with some of those
committees that clearly are of peripheral importance. What we

cannot understand is why our minister does not meet with *our* committee every month."

The delegation of authority and responsibility is one of the skills many ministers learn in order to facilitate a church growth strategy. This means a willingness to delegate *both* authority *and* responsibility. That often includes the authority to make a decision the minister might not wholeheartedly endorse. The slogan "I trust the people" must replace the desire "to be in on every decision."

This becomes a critical issue in the larger multiple staff churches where the senior minister must become comfortable with delegating both responsibility *and authority*. (In the very, very large congregation the typical response to this issue is to delegate to the paid staff, but not to volunteers.) Some senior ministers are willing to assign responsibility, but reluctant to delegate authority. One measure of this is when the senior minister can authentically affirm and applaud someone else's initiative and creativity in launching a new ministry or program, rather than second-guess a better way to have responded to that need.

Enabler or Initiator?

Perhaps the most popular leadership role to emerge for ministers during the past forty years is derived from the fourth chapter of Ephesians. Frequently this distinctive leadership role is summarized by such words as "equipper" or "enabler" or "coach." This concept of ministerial leadership was widely acclaimed in theological seminaries during the third quarter of this century and it has much to commend it. Experience suggests it does have some limitations. First, it requires a minister with a high energy level who has special gifts in helping individuals recognize their own gifts and talents. Second, it requires a high level of competence in a wide range of skills. Third, it requires a tremendous amount of time in one-to-one contacts, thus limiting its effectiveness either to congregations with fewer than two hundred members or to those larger churches content to have a large number of inactive members or to congregations with a comparatively large program staff. Finally, this leadership role for the pastor rarely results in significant numerical growth in congregations with more than a couple of hundred members. The enabler concept tends to be an inreach, not an outreach, leadership role!

Scores of pastors have discovered, often with great reluctance, that they had to abandon the enabler concept and accept a stronger role as an initiator if they were serious about the execution of a systematic new members enlistment strategy. These ministers not only had to be serious about evangelism; they also had to accept the responsibility for initiating and directing a program to turn the wish into reality. That was a pricetag for church growth.

The AAOEL Club

In addition to creating new Sunday school classes, perhaps an additional choir, an expanded worship schedule, and other new groups and organizations, an effective evangelistic effort often produces one other new group within the congregation. This can be identified as the AAOEL Club.

It is formed by those angry, alienated, and older ex-leaders who are unhappy with all the changes that have been made. They complain that they no longer know every other member, they are convinced the pace of congregational life is too fast, they know this church cannot afford all these new programs, they are unhappy about the increase in the size of the payroll, they are overwhelmed by the new complexity, and they long for the good old days.

While their numbers rarely exceed 1 or 2 or 3 percent of the membership, the members of this informal "club" (it usually meets without prior announcement in a member's home) often can be highly vocal in articulating their unhappiness with the growing sea of strange faces they see around them in church.

Some ministers attempt to enlist potential members of the AAOEL Club in helping to pioneer new programs and ministries, many try to "love 'em into silence," while others simply see this club as one of the inevitable price tags on an evangelism program that works.

While these five by-products of an effective evangelism effort are widespread, they do not constitute the whole list. Ministers who are serious about church growth also must face perplexing issues and questions. What do I neglect when faced with competing demands on my time? Associational and conference obligations? The local ministerial association? My family? My own personal, spiritual, and professional growth? How can I learn to be comfortable with complexity when the first churches I served taught me the joys of simplicity? How do I blend new leadership with old? How do we fit new programs into an already overcrowded building? What are the priorities I should have in mind when seeking new staff? How do we deal with the fact that in the numerically growing congregation the increase in financial support often lags behind the growth in membership and participation?

One response is to recognize these as normal and predictable consequences of an effective evangelistic effort. It always helps when you can describe yourself and what you are experiencing as normal.

A second response to this basic issue was illustrated by this conversation between Mary and Don Johnson one evening more than eleven years after they moved to St. John's Church. "Well," asked Mary, "have you decided what you want to do, move or stay here?"

"That's a tough question!" declared Don. "On the one hand I feel God is asking me to consider a new challenge, but I'm not convinced that I have finished what I've been called to do here at St. John's."

"Are you sure it's God who is asking you to take a new challenge," questioned Mary, "or do you simply have a case of itchy feet? A good many men about your age decide they have to prove to themselves they can still hack it out there. Some get a new wife. Others look for a new job or a new career. Preachers quite often start looking for a new church in order to prove to themselves they're still competent. Is it the call of the Lord or is it your own ego needs that's making you keep this other church believing you're interested in becoming their new senior minister?"

"To tell you the truth, Mary, I'm not sure," admitted her husband. "We've come a long way here at St. John's in eleven years. We've reversed what was a numerical decline, and worship attendance is now more than 50 percent higher than it was when we came here. We've built up a good staff and we've greatly expanded the program and outreach. Maybe I have done all I can do here and it would be good for St. John's to have a new minister come in and help them write the next chapter."

"Sounds to me as if you're trying to talk yourself into moving," reflected Mary, "and I believe you can do it. You talked me into marrying you and you talked yourself into coming here eleven years ago so I expect you can talk yourself into moving if that's what you want to do."

"Well, it's more complicated than that," continued Don in a thoughtful tone of voice. "I've changed a lot in these eleven years. When I came I was determined I did not want to be a domineering leader. I wanted to be part of a lay-clergy leadership team. I remember when I met with the committee a couple of them said St. John's needs a minister who is willing to be *the* leader here. I resisted that vigorously and their insistence almost persuaded me not to come. Now I am more comfortable with the idea of the pastor being the number one leader in a congregation. I think I'm that here today."

"You sure are!" interrupted Mary. "I don't think there's any question but you're the leader of this congregation today, and I think most of the people here are delighted with that. I'm convinced that your willingness to lead, to initiate new ideas and to be an innovator is the basic reason behind St. John's growth."

"Yes, and that growth has had its price tags," declared Don. "In fact, if you get right down to it, those price tags on our growth have been more than I expected to pay. I guess that's really why this chance to move is so attractive. It's not simply a bigger church or more staff or a better salary or a chance to move closer to your mother. The number-one attraction is the chance to start over again with a fresh slate. While I'm sure the overwhelming majority of the members at St. John's support me and my ministry, there have been more complaints and griping about petty things than I think can be justified. I'm not sure I need to put up with that anymore. I guess that's the real reason why I'm open to a move."

"Wherever you go, you'll always find at least a few people who love to nitpick and to complain about petty matters," observed Mary.

"That's true," agreed Don, "but in a fresh start I begin with a zero load of that baggage. Here I've accumulated more of that than I want to carry. You go on to bed, I'll be up later. I'm going down and begin to work on my resignation statement." With that remark, Don Johnson made it clear that the price of change and growth included his resignation. Chalk up another victory for the AAOEL Club. The members often think of themselves as losers in a lot of battles, but their persistence enables them to win quite a few wars.

SIXTEEN

THANKING THE PASTOR'S WIFE

.

Mary, I've never told you this before, but you've meant so much to me during these years," explained Helen Burt, an older member at St. John's Church. The occasion was a Tuesday evening farewell party for Don and Mary Johnson. After nearly eleven years as the pastor of St. John's Church, Don was about to become the pastor of another congregation and the moving van was scheduled to arrive early Thursday morning. This was the last in a series of farewell events various groups at St. John's had planned for the Johnsons.

When they returned home later that evening, Don said to his wife, "Mary, I didn't know you and Helen Burt were such good friends. I was surprised at the intensity of the emotion in her voice and the tears in her eyes when she said goodbye to us tonight. I never realized before that she saw you as a close friend."

"I was as surprised as you were," replied Mary. "I've always admired Helen for the life she has lived. Being widowed in your later thirties with three children to raise, the way she was, and working as hard as she has all her life must not have been easy, and I do admire her for what she's done, but I must confess I did not know she saw me as such a close friend."

"There's no question in my mind about her sincerity,"

observed her husband. "It was pretty clear from what she said that she will miss you more than she'll miss me after we leave."

"You know, Don, after eleven years I'm going to miss this house," declared Mary as she and Don were packing the next morning. "There are a few things about it I can do without, but it really has been a comfortable home."

"Oh, but day after tomorrow we move into our own home for the first time since we've been married," replied Don. "Although it's a few months early, think of that as my silver wedding anniversary present to you."

"That will be nice," declared Mary with a big smile, "but what I'm really going to miss when we leave here," she added in a voice that reflected a change in mood from happy anticipation to serious regret, "is moving away from all my friends in the Survivor's Club. It was nine years ago next month when some of us mothers who were living with a teenager for the first time decided to get together and form a mutual support group. We've been meeting together one evening a month for nearly nine years. It began with five of us, grew to about fifteen or sixteen and then as a few moved away, it dropped back to about nine, but we've become a very close group. All three of my closest friends are part of that group. Two of them no longer have teenagers, but we've stayed together as a group because we mean so much to one another. I'm really going to miss those dear friends when we move!"

* * *

"We were going to do a study of the responses of pastors' wives to the role expectations of the congregation and our methodology included polling a 10 percent sample of all of the pastors' wives in the denomination," explained a national staff member in one of the larger Protestant denominations. "When we got to that part of the research project we discovered no one had a list of the names and addresses of the women married to ministers in our denomination. We instruct all of our congregations to keep an up-to-date list of all their members in order to care for their people. We urge that whenever a pastor moves to a church, he or she study the membership roster in order to get acquainted with the names of the members. We tell them that if you don't know your people by name, you can't be a good pastor, but when the time came that we wanted to write some of the women married to our pastors, we didn't have a list of their names and addresses. I guess that says something about how serious is our concern for pastors' wives."

* * *

These three conversations illustrate three different ways we say "Thank you!" to the minister's wife. First, many of us, like Helen Burt, wait until just before we move away before we express our gratitude. Second, frequently we are completely unaware of what the minister's wife may have given up to move here with her husband, so we rarely express our gratitude for any sacrifices she may have made. We assume that if it was an attractive move for her husband, it must have been equally attractive for her. Likewise when the time comes to move on, we may not realize this means she must, on someone else's initiative, break some very close friendship ties.

Third, in several denominations, so little attention is paid to ministers' wives that no one has a complete list of them all by name and address. That may be a subtle way of saying, "Thank you for being willing to remain anonymous."

A Beginning Point

Where does a congregation begin to learn to say thank you to the minister's wife? One national authority on the subject of ministerial placement advises pastors, "If a congregation seeking a new minister asks you to come for an interview, inquire if your wife is invited. If that congregation does not invite her to participate in the interview process, or is unwilling to pay the travel costs for her to come along, don't go! If they do not appreciate the importance of her role and the value of her participation in the placement process, they probably are not prepared to accept the other responsibilities that go along with selecting a new pastor. If your wife does not want to participate in the interview, it is a free country and she has a right to say no, but in today's world no congregation has the right to exclude her by their unilateral decision."

The translation of that piece of advice is that the beginning point for a congregation's expression of concern for the pastor's wife begins before they meet her. It begins with the simple courtesy of including her as an important part of the ministerial placement process.

Housing

A closely related beginning point is in housing. While there has been a rapid increase in the number of congregations that provide a housing allowance, rather than a church-owned residence, for the pastor, most congregations with fewer than 500 members and many small town churches still expect the pastor to live in the parsonage or manse. One of the most significant expressions of interest offered by a congregation to the pastor's wife is to include her in all discussions on housing. While that may sound so obvious it does not merit mention here, it is a very sensitive point with many women who are married to a minister. As one of them said, "The members here knew we had this big red dog named Dan. When we arrived, we were surprised to discover the Men's Fellowship had built a very nice kennel for Dan. We spent at least two hours that first afternoon deciding on where to locate that dog house out in the back yard and in trying to be sure that Dan liked it. During the next several months I'll bet that at least a hundred different members asked how Dan liked his new house. It was almost a year later, however, before anyone ever asked me how I liked the parsonage. I guess my problem is I'm a brunette and Dan has red hair."

Some congregations respond to this issue by having two committees to be concerned with the parsonage. One is the trustees, or some similar group, that looks at the parsonage from a landlord's perspective. The second is the pastoral relations committee, and the members of that committee meet with the pastor's wife and look at it from the point of view of the persons living in it. Frequently there is a significant difference in these two perspectives!

A Contemporary Response

Recently several dozen women who are married to pastors were asked this question: How do the people in the congregation served by your husband say "Thank you" to you?

Three or four said that what they appreciated most was that at least a few of the members remembered their birthdays or wedding anniversary or some special day in the family's life together.

Several young mothers pointed out that from their perspective, the most important expression of appreciation was that the congregation provided free baby sitting services whenever needed. This was given special emphasis by one mother who said, "My husband serves three small congregations, one in town and two out in the country. All three congregations would like me to be present at many occasions and, while they are understanding if I don't show up, I know they feel a little neglected if my husband is there without me for some special event in that congregation's life. We have a two-year-old daughter and a five-year-old son and that could make it difficult. The third day after we arrived, however, a delegation of six people, two from each church, came to see me. One of them said, 'We have put together a team of ten people who will do baby-sitting for you at no cost. Carolyn here is in charge of this and whenever you need a baby-sitter, you call Carolyn. She'll find one for you. All we ask is that you type up a sheet of instructions and post it somewhere here in the house so that whoever is here will know what to do and what not to do. We know you're new here and wouldn't want to have to call a stranger, so you just call Carolyn and she'll find a reliable baby-sitter for you. It doesn't matter what the occasion is, whether it's something at one of the churches or to go somewhere with your husband or to go shopping, someone will be available. We also understand that occasionally you'll want an excuse not to go out, or there will be times when you prefer not to have an outsider with your children.' That is the nicest thank you I've ever received!'' observed this woman.

The most frequently stated response to this question, however, is illustrated by this statement from a thirty-nine-year-old woman married to a pastor in the American Lutheran Church. "The best thank you I receive from the people in the congregation my husband serves is they don't expect me to be the pastor's wife. I'm a member of the parish and I am treated very much like the other members. Several women are married to teachers, one is married to a physician, some are married to men who work in a big factory here, and I am married to a minister. I am treated as a person in my own right and no one places any expectations on me because I am married to their pastor. They address me as 'Anne' or as 'Mrs. Peterson,' not as 'the pastor's wife,' and they respect me as a person in my own right. That's the nicest expression of gratitude I receive!"

Another commented, "Although this may not fit your question, what I really appreciate in our present situation is the strong affirmation I receive as I pursue my career. I'm an attorney and I work in a law office seventeen miles from where we live. I'm a P.K. and I grew up in parsonages. My mother was the object of a lot of well-intentioned, but highly paternalistic, words and acts. I'm treated as a person who has a right to lead my own life and I appreciate that."

Another Response

When a parallel question was addressed on various occasions to seventeen lay men married to pastors, the responses varied, but none resembled those offered by women married to ministers. The closest to a consensus came from the man who said, "They don't say 'thank you' to me, here. They don't say much of anything. I don't think they know what to do with me or how to treat me." Although the world is changing, very few men married to ordained ministers see themselves in a situation comparable to those women who are married to pastors. The term "pastor's spouse" covers two separate but noncomparable categories. That is why this chapter is about saying "thank you" to women married to pastors.

.

SEVENTEEN

LEAVING A
LEGACY

If you want my opinion," offered Mary Johnson to her husband late one Tuesday evening in early March, "I think you should tell the church council you're resigning to take another call before you announce it from the pulpit. As the elected officials of the church, they are entitled to advance information on something as important as this. If they first hear it in church on Sunday morning, they'll have to give offhand responses when people ask why you're leaving."

"I see your point," admitted Don, "but I would rather that everyone would know it at the same time and the best way to accomplish that is by a Sunday morning announcement."

"That's also a good way to ruin the Sunday morning worship experience for a lot of people," retorted his wife. "If fifteen minutes into the service you announce your resignation, how do you expect anyone to concentrate on the prayers or hymns or your sermon?"

"That's a good point," agreed Don. "Maybe what I should do is to wait until just before I pronounce the benediction and at that point announce my resignation."

"Let me tell you the right way to do it," urged Mary. "Let's invite all of the members of the church council and a few other officers over a week from tonight for dessert and conversation here at the parsonage. It'll be crowded, but we can squeeze

them all in. We'll have dessert at 7:00 and after about a half
hour of small talk you can drop your bomb. If they leave by 9:00
nearly everyone in the parish will know by 10:00 that night that
we're leaving. By the following Sunday this will be old news and
you can make the formal announcement from the pulpit and the
only people who will be surprised will be one or two visitors
who are here for the first time."

At 7:10 the following Tuesday evening twelve of the fifteen
members of St. John's Church Council, the president of the
women's organization, the treasurer, the superintendent of the
Sunday school, and three other leaders were crowded into the
living room of the parsonage. As they ate their dessert eleven
were wondering why they had been invited and what this was all
about while three were thinking this was a great idea and that
Mary and Don should do this more often. Two, who happened
to be sitting next to each other, had heard that afternoon from
staff members at St. John's that Don was about to resign to go
to another church. Each had been sworn to secrecy and thus
had difficulty carrying on a conversation with the other. One
was thinking about a meeting that he had to attend later that
evening and was busy trying to figure out a way both to be polite
and yet to be on his way before 8:00. The eighteenth member of
the group had discovered the mixture of fruit in the dessert
included pineapple, to which he had a mild allergy, and he was
trying to decide whether he should force himself to eat it or
leave it on the dessert plate.

"In case you're wondering why we invited you over tonight,"
began Don, "there are three reasons why Mary and I thought it
would be good for us to get together this evening. The most
obvious is that neither Mary nor I had any meetings scheduled
for tonight and we simply didn't know what we would do if we
didn't have a meeting to attend. Second, both Mary and I enjoy
your company and we thought it would be nice simply to invite
you folks over for an hour or two. Third, I thought you should
know in advance that next Sunday morning, just before the
benediction, I will be making the formal announcement that I
am resigning to become the senior minister of another
congregation."

"What? You can't do that!" protested one person followed immediately by a variety of objections from nearly everyone else in the room.

"I didn't think you would be this surprised," responded Don with complete honesty. "I thought I had dropped enough hints and clues that most of you would be expecting this. While we really do hate to leave St. John's, there are several reasons why this appears to be the right time to make a move. First, I believe I've done about everything I can do here and this may be the time for someone to come in and help you write the next chapter. My goal when I came was to see St. John's grow and for each of the past three years our worship attendance has averaged well over 300. Second, Mary's mother is seventy-eight years old and, as you know, recently had to move into a nursing home. The church we'll be moving to is sixteen miles from that nursing home and that's four hundred miles closer than we are here. Third, our oldest daughter, Laura, graduates from the state university in June and our younger daughter, Becky, graduates from high school in May. From their perspective this is a good time for us to move. Fourth, in November I'll be forty-nine years old, so if I want to move before retirement, I'd better do it soon. I think you all know that few churches want a minister who is past fifty."

"We do," interrupted the president of the women's organization and two members of the church council, all women in their late fifties. "We think that's young."

"Seriously," continued Don, "when this opportunity came along, Mary and I talked at length about whether we want to stay here until I retire or take one more pastorate. If I'm going to move, this could be my last real opportunity.

"Fifth," added Don as he continued with his rehearsed set of reasons, "Mary wants to go back to school and get a Master's degree in counselling and this will give her a chance to do this at a top flight school not far from where we'll be living.

"Sixth, about three months ago, Lillian West, the most valuable player on our staff team, came in and told me that her husband will be returning in September and they plan to move to Arizona. I don't think I could make it here without Lillian, so I'll let my successor pick her successor.

"Seventh, Mary and I have decided that after more than twenty years of living in parsonages, we would like to buy our own home and this move will allow us to do this."

"That's not a good reason," objected Betty White. "When you came to St. John's eleven years ago, we gave you a choice between housing allowance and parsonage and you chose the parsonage. I'm sure that if you're willing to reconsider your resignation, we can offer you a housing allowance."

As he continued with his rehearsed list and offered another five reasons why this was a good time to terminate the pastoral relationship with St. John's, Pastor Don Johnson illustrated a point made many years earlier by John Steinbeck. "When the virus of restlessness begins to take possession of a wayward man, and the road away from Here seems broad and straight and sweet, the victim must first find in himself a good and sufficient reason for going. This to the practical bum is not difficult. He has a built-in garden of reasons to choose from."[1] Like all other itinerant ministers, Don had his built-in garden of reasons to choose from as he sought to explain his resignation.

This is not bad. Every departing pastor would be well advised to offer at least a half-dozen reasons as to why the time has come to move. For some of the people at St. John's, Don's desire to be closer to where his mother-in-law would be living was sufficient justification for the move. For others the decision to move before he turned fifty made sense. Several were in full agreement and sympathy with Mary's decision to go to graduate school and they commended Don's affirmation of his wife's desires. A few agreed that ten to twelve years was long enough for a minister to stay in one place. A large number saw this as a substantial promotion and therefore, while they may have preferred continuity to change, they could understand Don's decision as a rational and wise choice.

In the lives of many parishioners, it is a disruptive event when a loved, trusted, and respected pastor leaves. Many of the people can make the adjustment to this change more easily if they are offered what to them appear to be persuasive reasons for the change. Since not every reason is persuasive to everyone, it may be helpful for the departing pastor to offer several from which each can choose the most persuasive.

After their guests had left that evening and they were cleaning up and rearranging the furniture in the living room, Mary said to her husband, "I was interested to note that while you listed a dozen reasons why you thought the time had come for us to move, you never mentioned the AAOEL Club. I think it would have been good for those who really want you to stay to have heard that. It really isn't fair for 3 percent of the members to be able to prevail over the other 97 percent."

"I thought about that," replied Don, "but there are two reasons why I didn't mention the AAOEL Club. First, I was afraid that might be seen as the only reason for my departure and it really is only one of several factors. Second, I don't want them to have the satisfaction of believing they forced me out. As you know, one member of the club was here tonight and another was represented by his wife. I don't want them to be able to take the credit for my leaving. If they do, all they'll do is use the practice they've developed to make life difficult for my successor."

Successor or Predecessor?

With this decision, to resign from St. John's to move to another congregation, Don Johnson not only reluctantly conceded a victory to the AAOEL Club, he also now had to live with two new roles. For eleven years he had been Pastor Case's successor, although this role had begun to fade away after Don's first couple of years at St. John's. Now he needed to begin to think of himself as the successor to the senior minister of eighteen years at a church four hundred miles from St. John's.

It was much more difficult for Don to think of the second new role, the predecessor to his successor. Every recently arrived pastor feels the presence of the preceding minister who served that congregation. Some pastors commend their predecessor for thoughtfully and carefully paving the way. Many, however, are tempted to criticize the predecessor's shortcomings or negligence or thoughtlessness. It is easy to focus on this individual who can be identified by name, who can be pictured in one's mind, who is referred to by parishioners with varying degrees of affection, and who can be blamed "for making my ministry more difficult."

It is easier for a pastor to think in terms of being someone's successor than to imagine being the next minister's predecessor. Yet with the exception of those who help to close a church, every pastor is someone's predecessor. Both ethically and pragmatically, the successor is the pastor's neighbor. What can a pastor do to express love for that neighbor of tomorrow? It may help to think in terms of categories of information a minister can leave behind for that successor:

1. *Records.* The most obvious legacy, and the one that most pastors will expect to find, is a good set of church records. The membership roll should be up-to-date. It should include the name of each member, the current address, the date when that person united with the congregation and whether he or she joined by baptism, confirmation, transfer, reinstatement, or some other mode. In several denominations these records are kept by a lay volunteer. In most large congregations, membership records are maintained by a paid staff member. Nevertheless, the departing minister should check to be sure that the membership roster is in order.

A constituent roster should include persons who identify with the congregation, but who are not carried on the membership roll. In many Canadian and some United States churches this list may be nearly as long as the membership roster.

If a picture directory has been prepared, a copy of the two most recent editions should be given to the new minister on or before arrival. A list of shut-ins and others who need special attention from the pastor should be available. In many respects, the most valuable list of names a predecessor can leave behind is that of prospective new members, but too often it is carried in the pastor's head, and no written record exists.

The new minister will be grateful for a roster of all leaders and workers. It should include a list of all officers and also a list of Sunday school teachers, ushers, and others with special responsibilities. As a general rule, charter members expect a little extra deference, so if today's membership roll includes any charter members, their status should be noted.

If a new building has been constructed during the past several years, the successor will find it useful to receive a list of the names of persons on the building committee. One reason this group deserves special attention is the widespread tendency for one or more members of the building committee to drop into inactivity after completion of construction. The new minister may be in a position to reactivate those former leaders by means of some active listening.

These ten financial records should be made available to the incoming minister: (a) last year's budget; (b) this year's budget; (c) if available, the proposed budget for next year; (d) the financial statement for last year; (e) the financial statement for this year to date; (f) the amount and repayment schedule of any current indebtedness, including accumulated unpaid bills; (g) the total expenditures on a year-by-year basis for the past twelve years; (h) the total receipts *from member giving* (excluding loans, rentals, etc.) for each of the past twelve years; (i) the amount given by each of the top twenty contributors last year (without names attached to the dollar figures); and (j) the sources of all benevolence giving, including special offerings, designated gifts, and budgeted items.

The attendance records should include (a) the average attendance at Sunday morning worship for each of the past twelve years; (b) the Sunday-by-Sunday worship attendance record for the past calendar year and to date for this year; (c) the average attendance for each Sunday school class; and (d) the average attendance for special services such as Sunday evening, the drive-in worship service, Easter, Christmas Eve, the annual meeting, and other special occasions.

A copy of the history of this congregation should be made available to the new minister. Several pastors have left to their successor a file, or a bound volume, of the bulletins for the past year and of each issue of the parish newsletter.

Ideally this bundle of a dozen different sets of records will be gathered by a group of lay volunteers, not the departing minister, and given to the successor either immediately on arrival or even before arrival. The greater the lay ownership in putting this package together, the more helpful those members can be to the new minister. In this area of responsibility, it is best if the role of the departing pastor is to cause it to happen rather than to do it.

2. *Real estate*. The second part of the legacy to the successor consists of items related to buildings.

A new minister should receive a key to *every* door that will lock in the building. Most older buildings have distinctive characteristics or idiosyncrasies, and the new minister should be advised about the doors that will not lock, the rooms that cannot be heated without overheating the rest of the building, the public address system that picks up the local fire department calls, and similar concerns.

If the congregation provides a church-owned residence for the pastor rather than paying a housing allowance, a committee should be activated that will clean and see to the necessary repairs and improvements that can be accomplished during the period of vacancy. The departing minister should choose to be honest rather than polite in giving this committee a *complete* list of all necessary repairs to the parsonage or manse.

If, as is increasingly common, the congregation pays a housing allowance rather than providing a church-owned residence, the departing minister could raise the question with the finance committee as to whether the allowance is adequate for a newcomer to purchase a home at current interest rates.

If the congregation owns a gymnasium, fellowship hall, or other building space that is used by nonmembers, the new minister should receive a list of policies and rules on the use of the facility and a schedule of the projected events for the next several months.

3. *The program*. A third area in which the departing pastor can leave behind a useful legacy for the successor is information

on the church program. A three- or four-page list might include (a) the strongest groups, classes, organizations, choirs, and programs; (b) proposals for new programs now in the planning stage; (c) the most important annual events, programs (such as the traditional format for Christmas Eve or the schedule for Easter Sunday), and celebrations; (d) the traditional role of the choir in corporate worship; (e) special observances and dates, such as the annual celebration of the congregation's founding; (f) the regular weekly schedule, including any seasonal changes; (g) the traditional responsibilities of any staff person (Does the associate minister always preach the Sunday after Easter? Who leads the worship experience on laity Sunday?); (h) special warnings on what is "off limits here"; (i) local traditions for weddings, funerals, baptisms, farewells to departing members, a rose on the altar for the birth of a baby, or installation services for new officers; and (j) comments on the distinctive responsibilities and roles of special program staff, both lay and volunteer.

4. *The community*. Again, this task might more effectively be done by a layperson, but the departing minister should attempt to ensure that the new pastor receives (a) a map of the community, preferably with homes of members spotted on it; (b) an economic and social statement about the community (often available from the local chamber of commerce or planning agency); (c) information about the local school systems, both public and private; (d) traditional expectations of that congregation in regard to the role of the pastor as a community leader; (e) a list of the churches in the community or neighborhood with a few comments about relationships between this congregation and each of the others in programming (such as a union Thanksgiving service); (f) any special local tax provisions for which the new minister may be held responsible; and (g) a list of community events and programs this congregation or its pastor or both traditionally has shared in, such as the baccalaureate program for high school seniors or organ recitals.

5. *Other people*. Perhaps the one possibility that produces considerable anxiety among the laity is that the departing

minister might leave for the successor an annotated membership file describing all the characteristics, problems, faults, weaknesses, and shortcomings of each member. Obviously that should be avoided!

The departing minister might consider, however, a few notes on individuals who possess unfulfilled potential or who see themselves in the line of succession for certain leadership positions or who hold community leadership responsibilities. Some new pastors also appreciate being advised, "You should know that Mabel Jones is Harold Brown's sister."

The most useful "list" in this category may be the creation of a committee that will take the initiative and spend a few weeks helping the new minister become oriented to the community and acquainted with the members. Too often the call committee disbands after planning the reception for the new pastor.

6. *Personal and family concerns.* Many new pastors will appreciate knowing whom the predecessor chose as family physician, dentist, baby-sitter, or automobile mechanic, and who services the parsonage plumbing.

Some pastors also leave behind a note on the vacation schedule they followed or the names of ministers who might fill the pulpit in an emergency. Others may suggest special recreational and holiday opportunities.

7. *Victories and defeats.* One of the most effective methods of helping the new minister gain a sense of the distinctive legacy left by the predecessor was accomplished by one pastor who left behind two lists. One was labelled, "The six most meaningful highlights of my ministry here." The other was headed, "My six most serious mistakes." To make such lists requires a considerable sense of personal and professional security on the part of the predecessor, but it can be very helpful to the new minister.

8. *Unsolved problems.* "I know that none of my predecessors had a pleasant relationship with this choir director, and I haven't either," reflected one minister to himself as he was preparing to leave, "but maybe my successor will be able to work out a better relationship." Substitute for "choir director"

such titles as custodian, organist, church secretary, associate minister, or director of Christian education, and that reflection covers thousands of situations.

If the departing minister is convinced that a serious and continuing problem exists, it may be appropriate to attempt to resolve it before leaving rather than passing that legacy on to the successor. This same generalization applies to that leak in the roof, the side door that won't lock, the annual deficit in the church school budget, or the need to rotate a long-term member out of a particular office. It often is easier for the departing minister to face these unpleasant situations than for the new pastor.

9. *Neighboring pastors.* One meaningful act by the departing minister could be to organize several neighboring pastors who promise to take the initiative in calling on the new minister. Few pastors take the initiative to meet their new ministerial neighbors.

10. *A healthy termination.* Whenever the pastor-parish relationship is terminated, some people feel a sense of loss and grief. In the case of most long pastorates, this grief may be so profound that it automatically casts the successor in an "interim pastor" role.

The departing minister often can reduce the unproductive dimensions of the termination by an early announcement of the decision to leave, by cooperation with the congregation's desire to plan an impressive good-bye party, and by a willingness to accept a farewell gift. The humble minister who gives the people only a week or two to adjust to the announcement and who refuses to participate in any farewell events may be helping to convert grief into a destructive response—with the successor becoming the recipient of those negative feelings. The congregation must be given time to recover from the shock of the announcement, to plan a farewell event, and to become adjusted to the fact that a change will be made. People, like horses, do not like to be surprised. Sometimes they react to surprises with destructive behavior.

Finally, a pastor should not use that last sermon as the occasion to unload years of pent-up hostility. That may be a therapeutic exercise for the departing minister, but it also undercuts the people's respect for the office of pastor—and the successor who will inherit that office inherits the attitude.

The task of preparing this legacy sounds like a big load to place on the departing minister. It is—and some will not accept it. Many will and should turn most of the work over to a lay committee. There is another value in this checklist, however. It also can be used by the prospective new minister as a resource in suggesting probable expectations for the members to consider as they prepare to welcome their next pastor.

1. Picking a New Pastor

1. Robert K. Greenleaf, "The Servant as Leader," *Journal of Current Social Issues* (Spring 1971), pp. 4-29. For a more extensive discussion of leadership roles and styles see Lyle E. Schaller, *Getting Things Done* (Nashville: Abingdon Press, 1986).
2. For an elaboration of the symptoms of passivity see Lyle E. Schaller, *Activating the Passive Church* (Nashville: Abingdon Press, 1981), chapter 2.
3. This reference to "paying the rent" is from James D. Glasse, *Putting It Together in the Parish* (Nashville: Abingdon Press, 1972), pp. 53-61.

2. Picking a New Parish

1. For a more extended discussion of the value of some of the questions suggested earlier in this chapter and for a more detailed analysis of the different types of churches and for detailed descriptions of several different types of congregations see Lyle E. Schaller, *Looking in the Mirror* (Nashville: Abingdon Press, 1984), pp. 14-37; and Lyle E. Schaller, *The Middle-Sized Church* (Nashville: Abingdon Press, 1985).

4. The Intentional Interim Pastorate

1. For an elaboration on the distinction betweeen leadership roles and styles see Lyle E. Schaller, *Getting Things Done* (Nashville: Abingdon Press, 1986), chapter 5.

5. The Pastor's Compensation

1. For a statement on why the church should not be run as a business see Lyle E. Schaller, *Looking in the Mirror* (Nashville: Abingdon Press, 1984), chapter 2.

7. Winners and Losers

1. *The North American Interchurch Study* is the report of a study of stewardship based on nearly 3,600 intensive interviews conducted in the United States and Canada. Dr. Douglas W. Johnson was the project director for this study, which was published by the National Council of Churches in November, 1971.
2. James D. Glasse, *Putting It Together in the Parish*, chapter 4.

8. Well, Pastor, What Do You Think?

1. A remarkably lucid book on this approach to leadership is Warren Bennis and Burt Nanus, *Leaders: The Strategies for Taking Charge* (New York: Harper & Row, Publishers, 1985).

9. I Need Help!

1. For a more extensive analysis of this type of congregation see Lyle E. Schaller, *The Middle-Sized Church* (Nashville: Abingdon Press, 1985), pp. 99-137.

11. Who's in Charge Here?

1. For an elaboration on the place of discontent in the process of planned change see Lyle E. Schaller, *The Local Church Looks to the Future* (Nashville: Abingdon Press, 1968), pp. 225-27; or Schaller, *The Change Agent* (Nashville: Abingdon Press, 1972), pp. 122-23.

12. Where Are the Visitors?

1. A useful introduction is Steve Dunkin, *Church Advertising* (Nashville: Abingdon Press, 1982). A variety of resources can be purchased from *Net Results*, 5001 Avenue N, Lubbock, TX 79412.

17. Leaving a Legacy

1. John Steinbeck, *Travels with Charley* (New York: The Viking Press, 1961), p. 3.